When I Was Young
I Loved School

Dropping Out and Hanging In

by

Children's Express

Edited by Anne Sheffield and Bruce Frankel

CHILDREN'S EXPRESS wishes to gratefully acknowledge the support of the Primerica Foundation which made this book possible, and Peter Goldberg, the foundation's vice president, whose vision it was.

Library of Congress
    Catalog Card Number: 88-63736

ISBN 0-9621641-2-7

Cover and book design by Jean-Claude Suarès
Printing by Einson Freeman, Inc.

Acknowledgment

The editors of this book wish to pay special thanks to Karen Zelermyer, the former program director of Children's Express, for her tireless efforts on behalf of this book. She worked on it from its inception: planning, visiting various cities, contacting school officials, and generally orchestrating the entire project.

We also wish to thank the teen editors—the work horses—whose dedication, enthusiasm, sensitivity and seriousness made this book a reality. Their thoughtful and often astonishing interviews cut to the tap root of the dropout crisis, and for that the teen editors deserve full credit for this book.

The teen editors devoted a large amount of their time to interviewing education experts, including: Judy Weitz, director of state and local affairs for the Children's Defense Fund; Eugene Lang, whose advocacy of guaranteeing college tuition to every student who wishes to attend college is becoming a national movement; Irving Harris, another activist businessman, whose foundation in Chicago provides funding for the pre-school care of children as an early form of drop-out prevention; and Dr. Ernest Boyer, formerly U.S. Commissioner of Education under President Carter; and Anne Rosewater, staff director of the U.S. House of Representative's Select Committee on Children, Youth and Families.

In addition, we wish to thank the many other educators, principals, school administrators and guidance counselors (see Appendix) for contributing their invaluable help, time and cooperation.

We also wish to thank Aaron Retica, a former CE editor and consultant, who contributed many astute comments.

Finally, we would like to express our enormous gratitude to all the teenagers and children who participated in the roundtables and the one-to-one meetings (see Appendix for their names; in the text, names have been changed). Without them there would be no book. We are indebted to them for their courage and their willingness to share with us their lives and feelings at the risk of facing their own pain and embarrassment. We hope they profited as much as we did from the experience. We thank them and wish them all success—in or out of school.

Following are the teen editors responsible for this book:

Julie Horowitz, Senior Editor

Rachel Burg
Glenn Golz
Thelma Foster
Linda Holmes
Adam Horowitz
David Katz
Maureen Macione
Meredith Miller
Tanya Pearlman
Elspeth Steiner
Rebecca Walkowitz
Jonathan Zachary

Thanks as well to the many other reporters and editors who contributed to it.

The only people for me are the mad ones, the ones who are mad to live, mad to talk, mad to be saved, desirous of everything at the same time, the ones who never yawn or say a commonplace thing, but burn, burn, burn like fabulous yellow roman candles exploding like spiders across the stars and in the middle you see the blue centerlight and everybody goes "Awww!"

—JACK KEROUAC

Contents

Preface

The title of this book indicates its intent: to go directly to the voice of the child, to listen to it, to let it speak about the conditions of life and education at the end of the twentieth century in America. The children and teens who speak share none of the polite distance of academic discourse. They claim none of the dispassionate, orderly objectivity of statistics. They almost warn us off, promising to reveal all of their pain and disappointment, to engage us in conversations where the child, not the adult, is the ultimate authority.

In early 1987, thirteen teenage editors of Children's Express set out to investigate this country's dropout crisis in the only way that made any sense: to talk—kid to kid—with teenagers who had quit school, with those who had returned to give it a second chance, and with others who were fighting against all odds to hang in there.

In teams of two, they traveled to five American cities—Newark, Boston, Kansas City, Dallas and Oakland—and, in school and out, interviewed hundreds of youths. They conducted and tape-recorded informal discussions with groups of students chosen spontaneously at each school they visited. They also had in-depth conversations with selected participants and with others they met elsewhere. Sometimes these one-to-one meetings took place at parks or even in the backs of cars because a parent refused to accept the Children's Express ground rule: no adults allowed.

The rate at which America's children drop out of school has received a lot of press: one out of every four high school students quits before graduation. Critics of our educational system have vividly underscored the risk this dropout rate poses to the nation's future. The message is now so clear and extensively documented that it should screech in the ear of every adult and be at least as infuriating and unsettling as one of those incessantly blaring car alarms that disturb our sleep, that wreck our nights, that contaminate our peace.

Disturbing facts about school children "at risk" have been marshalled time and again. Here is "A Day In The Lives of American Children," presented by the Children's Defense Fund:

1,868	teens dropout of school
988	American children are abused
2,989	children see their parents divorced
1,099	teenagers have abortions
1,287	teenagers give birth
110	babies die before their first birthday
27	children die because of poverty
5	school-age youths are murdered
5	teens commit suicide

Studies have established strong correlations between the dropout rate and such factors as poverty, abuse, teen pregnancy, the breakdown of the nuclear family. Poor children, for instance, are three to four times more likely to drop out than affluent children. Of the 562,100 teens who become mothers each year, four out of five will drop out of school for some period of time. Children living with only one parent are far more likely to leave school than children from intact families—sixty-eight percent more likely if living only with their mother and seventy-eight percent more likely if living only with their father.

Race, of course, remains a factor. The dropout rate for blacks has improved in recent years and, when all other factors such as income or the level of parents' education are removed, the rate is roughly the same as for white students. The problem is that almost half of all black children live in poverty, and their numbers are increasing.

The data concerning Hispanic children are particularly disconcerting. Up to eighty percent of inner-city Hispanics drop out of high school before graduation. Twenty-five percent of all Hispanic students are two years behind by the eighth grade, a significant figure when considered alongside findings that students who are kept back are the likeliest to drop out. Despite this enormous dropout rate, only a tiny fraction (3.2 percent) of all public school teachers who instruct Hispanic students have academic training to teach them.

The relationship between basic skills, teen pregnancy and dropping out is also staggering. Teens with poor basic skills are five times as likely to become mothers before the age of 16 as those with average skills. Some 1.2 million adolescent girls get pregnant annually at a 1987 cost to the U.S. taxpayer of $19.3 billion.

That, of course, is only one computation of cost. For dropouts, the likelihood of being unemployed, requiring welfare, remaining in poverty or going to jail increases dramatically when they leave school. They can expect, on average, to earn $441,000 less in a lifetime than high school graduates.

For those who leave school and turn to drugs and alcohol, delinquency and crime, the costs are truly beyond calculation. Our juvenile institutions are often little more than training grounds where all too often children enter as non-criminal "status offenders" and emerge equipped and ready to launch their criminal careers.

For society, the expense can be calculated several additional ways: Sixty percent of all dropouts are functionally illiterate. Currently one-third of all new enrollees in the U.S. military have not completed high school, and half of them weren't thought capable of completing their first tour of duty. The economic burden imposed on the nation's businesses to train workers—already calculated in the billions of dollars—may soon be crippling. The percentage of the workforce that is drawn from the poorest and least educated segment of the population is increasing while the total workforce continues to decline. Where once seventeen workers supported every retiree, only three will do so by the year 2000.

As troubling as these dropout-related statistics may be, they are in great competition with other grim statistics and, after all, are only numbers. The Children's Express teen editors wanted to learn about the lives behind the numbers. They sought, in the informal discussions and the subsequent meetings, to have conversations rather than to conduct interviews. As a result, their teenage peers, dropouts and students alike, willingly revealed their lives.

They talked about why they cut classes, why they do drugs, why they rebel. They make real what statistics don't: the father's fist, the mother's abandonment, the sale and use of drugs as available as candy, the unplanned birth of a child, the teacher's indifference, the schools that are as impersonal as prisons.

The teen editors also learned about how a child dreams in even the deadliest circumstances, about what stimulates, nurtures and strengthens, about the inspired teacher—too few of them—who makes the rare connection that stirs aspirations, instills confidence, and leads to learning and its rewards.

Many of those who talked about their lives said they had never discussed these matters with anyone, not even their friends. No one had asked, so no one had listened.

From thousands of pages of transcripts, we selected these twenty-three voices to speak for the rest. Also included are the voices of two adults, one

Preface

a high school principal who was himself a dropout, and one teacher on a unique crusade to give high-risk kids the means to save themselves.

The editors have added, too, the words of children and adults speaking through poetry, song and literature to punctuate the voices that emerge.

Children's Express, the New York-based news service reported and edited by young people, was founded by Robert Clampitt in 1975. It operates on the assumption that children have important ideas and deep concerns, but have limited avenues to express themselves, to communicate and to be taken seriously. It fosters children's self-esteem through participation in journalism, where they can integrate and express their own developing values, and, in so doing, realize they can make a difference.

The teen editors who made this book have worked after school, on weekends and during vacations. They believe that by removing the adult filters, they will contribute to the national dialogue by presenting a different, clearer and more complete picture of dropouts in America. They have tried to provide a new way of looking at this problem which is more human and humbling than the statistics suggest.

Teen editor Julie Horowitz once said of the kids of this book, "I felt like they were looking to me and saying, 'Listen to my life.'" We join the staff and the teen editors of Children's Express in thanking Primerica Foundation for allowing these children and teens the chance to be heard.

Anne Sheffield and Bruce Frankel

Part One

The Dropouts

We interviewed dropouts wherever we found them—parks, museums, bus stations —and whenever they came to us through friends or schools. We feel that it is foolish to generalize about them, to bunch them together under an umbrella of common characteristics. Even where similarities in their histories emerged—the lack of a stable, healthy family environment the most recurrent— we ended not with mere impressions of dropouts, but with vivid memories of unique individuals.

We interviewed Sheila at her mother's small apartment in a bustling, working-class section of Oakland. She was tall and strikingly beautiful, with partially bleached shoulder-length hair. She was dressed in the chic style of a Bay Area cafe waitress, which, at the time, she was. She was vibrant, exciting, sharp and seemingly happy.

We ran into Brent at the Children's Museum in Boston and interviewed him there inside an Indian wigwam. His long black hair was partially covered by a blue bandanna fitted around his head. A metal chain hung around his neck, a silver cross dangled from one ear and he wore a denim jacket on which "LICK ME" was emblazoned in bold black letters. He was proud that he had dropped out of school, that he had rebelled against an institution he said tried to deprive him of his right to free speech.

Sara, a 15-year-old from Berkeley, dropped out of high school because she was bored with her classes. She is free-spirited, delightful and dauntless. She is also rebellious and curious, and almost convincing in her dismissal of school's importance.

In Newark, the school system's guidance department kept a log of all students who had dropped out during the previous twelve months. Postcards were mailed, inviting dropouts to talk with us. Mario, a young Hispanic who lives at home with his mother and sister, showed up at the board of education's office. He was accompanied by a girlfriend who had recently gone back to school after dropping out.

The day was chilly and gray as we sat on the ground and talked with Marybeth and Juliet in Martin Luther King Park, known as Provo Park, across the street from Oakland's enormous Berkeley High School. Often during our interview drug dealers tried to sell us marijuana and other drugs. Marybeth had brought her own and rolled a joint while she talked.

One of us had grown up with Marybeth and been a close friend until about eighth grade. Her life had not seemed that different then. Without any apparent reason, Marybeth changed. She began to cut school and take drugs. Her style of dress, as on the day we talked, became cheap and provocative. She no longer spoke as she once had, but adopted the dialect of the tough and streetwise.

Marybeth brought her friend, Juliet, along to the interview. Juliet looked colorless and drained, as if life had already siphoned much out of her. She was pregnant, though not yet showing, and painfully alone. Afterwards, we visited the building where she stayed. It was cold, had no electricity, and possibly no running water. It was difficult to see how she would ever have the resources to get her life on track.

Teen Editors: *Julie Horowitz*
Tanya Pearlman

The Dropout

13

Many times I've been alone
And many times I've cried
Anyway, you'll never know
The many ways I've tried

—from "The Long and Winding Road"
JOHN LENNON AND PAUL MCCARTNEY,

Sheila, 17

"When I was young I loved school."

The Dropout

When I was young I loved school. I was so good in school that my mom trusted my judgment. If I said I didn't want to go, she said, "Okay. You know." I've been through so many different schools. There were a couple of times where I'd switch schools three times in one year, even in the first grade.

That was hard. But in a way it was good. I learned how to adjust and meet people really easily. There's nothing more horrifying than when you have to go into a new school and you don't know anybody. Everybody's looking at you. But that doesn't faze me anymore.

In eighth grade I started cutting school. It was kind of fun, you know. I got in a lot of trouble. I wasn't there enough. When I fell behind, I got frustrated. But I did all right. I got straight A's.

In the ninth grade I really started fucking up. They were threatening my mom. If I didn't go to school, they were going to fine her fifty days in jail or something like that. She got all freaked out. That's why she finally said, "Well, why don't you go to your dad. I don't want to go to jail."

My dad used to beat me up pretty bad. I had bruises. I wouldn't go to school because I was afraid. What could I say? "Oh, I got in a fight." Five fights a day?

I wouldn't go to school when it was real bad. I was afraid because nobody believed me. My dad was like Mr. Nice Cop. "Oh, he wouldn't do that!"

He's a big guy, right? He's like 6'4" and two hundred pounds. Lifts weights and stuff. He beat me for fifteen minutes on my ass. I had broken blood vessels all over. I couldn't sit down and I had bruises on my face.

I finally went and told the school nurse what happened. They got me a social worker. I told them, "Don't say anything to him. Don't confront him until you get me out of the house." They said, "Okay, okay, don't worry."

The motherfuckers told him, called him and let him know. He came home and beat the shit out of me. He kicked my door in. I locked my door, because I knew that he was going to come in. I was so scared, I was hiding. Finally, I got away.

Sometimes I wonder how my dad feels.

He just pretends I don't exist now. I mean, I am his only kid. But I guess he doesn't care either. For a long time I did. For a long time, it was real hard. But now, I don't care.

I moved to California at the end of August, two Augusts ago. I went to Berkeley High. I liked it. I was really impressed by all the opportunities you had there and all the different choices you had. It was stimulating.

The Dropout

But after I met people and I started having a social life and everything, I'd miss my morning classes a lot. I wasn't really living at home. I was living wherever. And I was taking lots of acid. My boyfriend at the time wasn't really doing anything for himself. He wasn't going to school. And I just kind of stopped going.

We ended up running away. We went down to Carson and got as far as Santa Barbara before the cops got us. This one cop said, "I'm going to make sure the two of you never see each other again."

They sent me to the survival school, which was fucking hell. It was intense, the most intense experience I've ever had. No baths, no change of clothes, no change of underwear for three weeks. And no food for three days. Hike ten miles a day with a forty pound backpack on, through sand, up mountains. You didn't see any sign of civilization for three weeks.

It was in the winter. There was snow on the mountains. No tent, no sleeping bags, just a blanket. You had to dig these little ditches at night for your bed. You would dig a hole and you would put hot rocks in it, then cover it back up with dirt. There were six of us there. Side by side, we looked like six level graves.

People got so hungry they ate mice. I'm not lying. They ate ants. I mean, it was really intense. I'm a vegetarian. No thank you, I'll pass.

Education is really important to me. My mother has stressed that my whole life. I think from the time I was born, she said, "You're going to get an education." That's just been pounded into me, right? That's probably the only thing that I listened to. The only thing.

I just didn't want to be in a classroom. There's a lot to learn, but you can't learn in the classroom.

I started taking drugs when I was so young. The first time I ever smoked a cigarette, I was ten. The first time I smoked pot, I was ten. The first time I took acid, I was twelve. I've done just about everything, I think.

I remember a time when I said I'll never stick a needle in my arm. I truly believed that. I don't know what it was, I got into this—it sounds so sappy to say—live-for-the-moment thing. Yeah, just take everything as it comes. I was just . . . spontaneous. I loved it.

I'll try anything once. But I never thought that I would become a goddam strung-out junkie. That's kind of incredible.

I look back at myself when I was in the seventh grade. I was such an intellectual. I was such a good girl then. I was like everybody's babysitter. Everybody trusted me.

The Dropout

19

I've done so many things that if I was a mother, I wouldn't know what to do. I'd want to be there, but what the hell do you do when your baby's a junkie?

I'm so glad that I turned out the way I am instead of this little white, suburban rich kid that didn't know anything. I'm thankful that I ended up like this instead.

I don't consider myself a dropout. 'Cause I'm not. I'm not a dropout. I'm not quitting, you know? I have no intention of stopping. Because there's so much more. Right now, I'm just taking a temporary pause.

I feel like needles and drugs and being addicted—it sucks the soul right out of you. You become such an empty shell, you know? I had really good friends. We'd get high together and stuff. But they just got swallowed up. It's real sad to me. I think it's also hard because I let a lot of people down when I was on drugs. When you're on drugs like that—shooting up heroin and speed and coke—it's all real addicting, and that's all you think about. I let a lot of people down, and that was no fun. I flaked on everybody all the time. It took a lot to get back the trust I lost.

I got down to ninety-six pounds. I was so unhealthy, I looked like shit. And then I knew that I had to quit—I had to. I really want to have kids some day. I really do. I just started thinking in terms of the future. Because I didn't think about the future ever. I just thought about now.

Now that I keep the future in mind, it makes a big difference. A big difference. I'm going back to school. I don't want to quit school. Even when I quit school before, I knew that I would never be a dropout. I want to be educated. And I still want to go to college. I still want to be a veterinarian.

You know, sometimes it scares me, because I think, God, could I do it? Can I do it? I can't even get up in the morning. How are you going to go to fucking school when you can't even get up in the morning? They're not going to go for that. But I'm going to try.

The Dropout

Excuse me for living,
I'm sorry I dared step foot
on this earth.
Don't blame me,
it's not my fault.
If you don't want me here
then life's not worth living
anyway.
So excuse me,
I know when I'm not wanted.
I'm calling.
Hey, I'm calling you,
can't you hear?
Don't you know I'm
alive?
Why don't your eyes
ever search for mine?
I love you.
Hey, I'm calling you.
I just said
I love you,
can't you hear?

—TONYA PENDLETON, 12

Brent, 18

"I quit school because of the way I thought, the way I dressed, the way I was..."

The Dropout

23

I was eighteen and a senior when I dropped out three weeks ago. I used to get harassed by the teachers and the whole student body because I was different. People couldn't deal with that. Most people look at me and call me a punk, which I don't mind. But I don't totally like it.

What would I call myself? Myself. Just being me.

Mom was kind of expecting it. All this year I was getting harassed by the vice principals and the principal. Everybody treated me like a criminal. I think they eventually started getting a little bugged by the fact that they couldn't get me, you know, suspend me or anything. I wasn't doing anything wrong. So they had every teacher keep an eye on me. I couldn't walk down the hall without having one teacher follow me and having another teacher watching from the other end of the hall. It was like they had all these little walkie-talkies. They didn't. That was just the atmosphere I was dealing with.

At first I thought that the system was out to get me. And then I thought it over again. I said, "No, maybe it's just me and I'm making everything up."

I was in all the average classes. I was lazy. I didn't like doing school work, even though I had the brain power to do it. School was boring. And the school work I was learning was boring. Boring, boring, boring. That's it. I feel right now like I know more than I was going to learn this year in my classes. So, you know, I think I have the intelligence.

It's not really what they're teaching. Some people like me, they're intelligent on their own. They don't buy their education. They just have it. You're sort born with intelligence. Some people are, some aren't.

You find all these college professors and everything like that. They went to all the best schools in the world to get their PhD's and this and that. You know, they gained it in school, and it's like they buy it. They don't have it to start.

Did I ever cut classes in school? Not much. That's one of the things that bugged the school. I wasn't doing anything wrong. And they were getting kind of frustrated because they couldn't bag me for anything.

Last year I got suspended a lot. Every year I used to get suspended at least two or three times, which I didn't consider a big deal. But this year, nothing happened until the situation with the librarian where I told her she was a pain in the groin. They suspended me for ten days. And "groin's" not even a profanity. That was really an unfair way to treat me. That's when I decided it wasn't worth it.

It was like a prison. I couldn't be who I wanted to be. Prisoner of thought, prisoner of conscience. I quit school because of the way I thought, the way I dressed, the way I

The Dropout

24

was, the way that was easiest for me to be. I'd graduate this year and do my music, but now I have a chance to start it earlier. I'm trying to look on the bright side.

I miss it a little bit, the teachers that were cool and kids that were cool. There were a lot of kids that I never really liked, but they sort of looked up to me because I was being me. And I kind of miss that. It's like your own following. I can always gain that elsewhere.

Right now the future looks pretty bleak. I've been playing music for a few years now and I think I have a future in it. So I'm going to stick with that. Be a musician.

My brother was a dropout. My real father was a dropout. It's a very upsetting term. I don't think it applies to me. That's why I look at it in a humorous way—to sort of lighten up the mood of the situation.

My older brother is a good example. He's not doing a thing with his life. He dropped out of school three years ago. Three or four years ago, and he's not doing anything. He's had about twenty-five jobs. He's never been able to hold a job long. He's probably going to end up in jail pretty soon for fines he hasn't paid. And for a lot of drugs. You know, that's what I see as a stereotypical dropout.

You have to know why you're dropping out of school. You can't just drop out if you've got nowhere to go, nothing to do. A person—if he really wants to drop out and he's in the same situation as me in school—then I'd say, sure, as long as you want to do it. I mean, I can't say no.

My folks are all right, although right now they're kind of nagging me to get a job. I don't see my parents as having failed. I see the school system as a failure.

Right now, I just record and write. You can see anger in my music. You can see frustration. Most of the songs are about peace. Peace, freedom and the proverbial love song. Everyone has to have at least one or two love songs in order to get by. So I've got a couple of those. I think most of my music is basically angry at the whole world, at the whole situation of life and reality.

When I first went to school—I can remember the first day I went to school—I hated it. I didn't want to be there. But I started seeing things in school that I liked, like reading. You know, I could actually feel my brain getting more intelligent, which was one of the things I thought was pretty cool.

Eventually, I kind of put the books down and didn't let anybody see that I read because everybody would think I was a little wimp. My big kick was beating up on other people. This whole stage of life was when my parents were breaking up. So I was angry as a little kid, beating up other kids.

The Dropout

I used to go home and I'd read a book. I always kind of liked school. I could learn. But I always sort of hated it, too, 'cause we were forced to do it. I mean, I learn on my own.

I've always planned to be a musician. That was one of the reasons why I wanted to get my diploma. But now, if that's what people are going to judge me on, then I'll let them. I'm going to do my own thing.

I'd like to get a good college education. But college is nothing like high school. It's not as structured. One of the problems with first grade through twelfth grade is the structure of it. You're forced to learn. I mean, if you want to take these courses in college, you don't have to show up. It's your fault if you fail the course.

School should be like college. Open campus, open this, open that. They shouldn't force kids to go to school. And then when you grow up and you see more of the moral decay of the whole society you say, wow, I should have gone to school. You know? It should be your own burden, not somebody else's.

At least high school should be like college. It shouldn't be like fifth grade. The ideal high school would be just like a college. You go to what class you want and you take what classes you want and learn what you want. You can do your homework if you want to. If you find out late in life that you're failure, you can blame no one but yourself. In my situation, I look at it more like I was driven out of school.

If you think that dropping out of school is best for you, then that's what you should do because you'll feel more happy about it. I admire anybody that does what they want. People who are being what they want to be, we can relate to them. No matter what, as long as they're not trying to preach things.

The problem is the dropouts who don't know why they dropped out. I know why I dropped out, so I'm not a problem. I think dropouts are problems, like my older brother, a druggie getting in trouble with the law.

I'm an exception. I know why I did it.

I don't think I'll ever look back. I've moved around a lot. Since I was a little kid, I've been to about ten different schools. Every school has its own method of teaching, and after six or seven schools I had to form my own thought process. Most teachers are stuck in their own beliefs. They preach, they don't teach. And I eventually taught myself. I took the book home and I taught myself. That's why I don't think I'll ever look back and wish I didn't drop out of school.

The Dropout

26

We busted out of class; had to get away
from those fools.
We learned more from a three-minute record (baby)
than we ever learned in school.
tonight I hear the neighborhood drummer sound;
I can feel my heart begin to pound.
You say you're tired and you just want to close your eyes
and follow your dreams down.

—"No Surrender"
BRUCE SPRINGSTEEN

Marybeth, 15

"It's like half of me is grown up and half of me isn't, because I just jumped out of my house too soon."

The Dropout

I was born in Berkeley, way down in the boondocks, down on Tenth Street. I grew up with my mother and father. I was happy but I was poor. I had a good childhood, real music and art-oriented. Both my parents have a lot of education, and they traveled a lot. They were real liberated people. They taught me to have good morals about people, about good and bad, love and learning to care about people and the right things to do. I got a lot of love and support to do what I wanted to do, encouragement to go to school, to be a creative person.

My parents separated when I was seven. I didn't get along with my father, so that was good, because I stayed with my mother mostly. My dad and I just didn't get along, characterwise, you know? We never did. He's a really good father, but he's really opinionated.

Up until I was thirteen it was wake up, go to school, walk home, eat dinner, do my homework and go to sleep. On the weekends we watched Saturday morning cartoons. It was just total family. On Sunday we'd go on an outing. But then, all of a sudden, I started doing more things, being really rebellious, leaving the house, staying out late, all the typical stuff. Getting grounded, being trouble.

School has always been important to me. In junior high I got straight A-pluses. I was smart. I got A-pluses up until last semester. If I got an A-minus I would have a tantrum because I had a high standard for myself. I can't bear to squeak by with D things. I just can't stand it. You get criticized, and I don't like criticism of myself. I have a real high standard.

I started flaking out in school. I would go and just talk to my friends or write notes or get high and get burnt. I don't really mind learning, if I'm talking with somebody and they're telling me something interesting. It's different. But when you sit in this classroom, it's so, how do you say, societal. It's just like society. It's sitting in a classroom with this person teaching you, pointing to the blackboard, and all these people sitting behind their desks. I don't know. If there was a different way to learn or a funnier way, I'd do it in a minute.

If the teachers are interesting, the learning is interesting. If they're into it and they like it, if they're enthusiastic about it, then it rubs off on the class. If they're boring teachers, who's going to sit there and listen to some—I don't mean to be mean—some "old man?" Somebody just boring, period, who doesn't make it interesting, who just says this is what happened in this year or that year, not how it happened and why it happened and what caused it and how people must have felt about it.

The Dropout

So, when I was thirteen I started partying and stuff, trying to be cool, be with all my friends. I was just having fun because I was meeting new people. Gradually, I started doing worse in school.

I changed over the summer, between eighth and ninth grade. I met Tasha. We became really good friends. And she was all into going out, having a good time, and she didn't really care about school or anything. She got me into partying and drinking and such, so she was my bad influence. Now she's back in school, doing really well.

So, of course, it was more than Tasha. It was me. I just play it by ear so much, I wasn't thinking about what I was doing. It's like the whole time I knew I was doing the wrong thing by going out of school, but at the same time I started to care less and less. And pretty soon I just wanted to stop altogether.

Then I met my boyfriend, and he just kind of swept me off my feet before I even had a chance, really, to go back. My boyfriend thinks I should go back to school. He cares a lot about school. But by the time I met him I was practically not going to school at all. By the time I met him, I didn't even care anyway. And then he got me into smoking weed, right?

I was smoking weed, a little bit, but not to an extreme when I met him. Then I started smoking weed, and it messed me up. I still smoke a lot but I keep it more under control. One thing I can say for myself, I don't do cocaine. I never liked it, never would. There are tons of people in Berkeley, and half of them are coke fiends. I tried drinking for a while. That was fun. But it never went down very well, alcohol. So I don't even do it. You know, maybe a beer every now and then.

I tried acid once. But I kept it under control, because I have a lot of self-respect, and I don't want to hurt my body. I always ate really good food no matter where I was, you know, to keep healthy. And sometimes I get fat.

So gradually, I got more and more into marijuana, okay? At first, I was just smoking weed, sitting on my ass in Provo Park, doing nothing, just stuck in the middle of whether I wanted to stay at home, go to school, or do my thing and be with my boyfriend.

I'll tell you, when you start smoking a lot of weed, it becomes an important thing to you. You get sucked into it. Everyone I know who smokes a lot of weed sells it also.

For the last six months I've decided what I want to do. I've been trying to deal, you know, with the responsibility of being an adult. I've been having to make my living, buy my own food, dealing with people way older than me. Dealing with a lot of drugs because my boyfriend is twenty-five years old, and he's been through a lot. Really. His whole family is totally into drugs, and that totally changed my life. I just hate his house.

The Dropout

31

Right now, I have tantrums sometimes. Like I feel like a little baby. It's like half of me is a grown-up and half of me isn't, because I just jumped out of my house so soon. I can't do both. I can't go to school and stay at home and be with him, at the same time. He's really not welcome in my house. I was stuck between being at home or moving out.

My boyfriend kind of led me astray, so I was hardly at home. I totally fell in love with him. I want to be with him. At the same time, I want to stay home and go to school. But I jumped into his world completely and now it's like I don't know if I could ever go back to living at home.

Me and my mother aren't getting along very well, just going through the usual rebellious stuff. And I've done so much stuff to wrong her, stealing things and all.

Before I wasn't thinking about what I was doing. Now I do. Now I'm thinking about what I'm going to do.

Right now what I want to do is get an apartment for myself. I'm going to be staying at my mother's for a couple of weeks until I get enough money to get an apartment, to get a job. I've been selling weed, which seems really bad, but it's not like big-time drug dealing. I've just been, you know, trying to make some money. I won't even mess with coke, really. I'm just selling weed, you know?

I did get a job a while ago. I worked my ass off. I got fired. I was so mad. I worked for five days, forty-four hours. This was in a cookies and ice cream place. They were real preppy and straight at this place, and they just didn't like me from the beginning. They didn't trust me, either.

One time I messed up on the job. The boss would be there, and they'd all be looking over my shoulder and making me nervous. I messed up on the change twice. You know, by giving someone ten dollars more than I was supposed to. I caught it, I caught my mistake, but still I got fired. I got fired from the job, but I know I can always go out and get myself another one.

Finally it got to the point where I just couldn't live at home anymore and I wanted to be with my boyfriend so bad. I had to get my own place. So I've been working trying to make money. I've been putting like fifty dollars every other day, whether from this work or from weed. I can make a hundred dollars a day selling weed if I want to. Like I got my paycheck, I just bought a big batch, a hundred and fifty dollars of some really nice weed, and just sold it.

I've chosen a risky kind of path to take in my life. Ever since I was thirteen, I've been stuck in the middle, between staying in school, doing what I was supposed to do, and trying to be an adult.

The Dropout

32

But I'm getting it together, because I made a promise that I'm going back to school, at least for two more years. You know, there are options. You can take the GED and go to a junior college. You can go to night school. You can go to continuation school. As soon as I get an apartment, as soon as I get settled in a house, I'm going to enroll in school again and try to work part-time.

I regret taking the path I've taken, but that's the way things worked out. It's the only way. Because half of me grew up so fast. You know what I'm saying? It was like I feel worn down, or I feel drained. I chose to deal with adult responsibilities way sooner than I had to.

The biggest change happened when I met my boyfriend six months ago, but it was gradually happening before then, too. It's not just one thing. I got impatient with school, and I met so many people, and I started just getting out in the world. I was realizing there's so many things you could do besides school. I'd been working so hard all those years, I just all of a sudden started getting more and more lazy, as far as school went. It's made me feel real bad about myself, and it's made me treat other people real bad, too. Because you know, when you feel like shit about yourself you treat other people like shit.

I knew I was wrong all the time. It's just not a thing that a fifteen year old girl is supposed to do. But at the same time, I've had a lot of fun. I may regret it, but I'm still the same person, and I still love my parents, my family. I still want to do something with life. I may have chosen another path, but I'm still the same person, you know, and I still look at people the same way. I feel I know good from bad.

What's a typical day in my life? Everyday they change, but for a while it was just in the park. Provo Park is a place with a lot of people, a lot of friends. It's drug-oriented. The whole park is drug-oriented. It's dropout. It's just to get high, basically. The park is to get high and meet your friends. Everyone passes through the park. They'll go to Berkeley High and they'll come here and they'll get high for a couple of years, and then they'll go on with their lives and get it together somehow. Maybe they'll regret it, you know, but they'll get it together eventually. And then there are a few of them, like my boyfriend, who just stuck around here for ten years when he wasn't in prison for white slavery and twenty-one counts of selling an ounce of weed to an undercover cop who went to Berkeley High. Now, I know my boyfriend sounds like a scumbag. This is what he told me.

Before I was on this rebellious trip, I didn't care about anyone or myself. I just wasn't thinking, but now it's like I really want to do something with myself.

Education has always been important to me. It has been for a long time. For the last couple of years, every time I've tried to start over and do it again, I just mess up. I got lazy. I don't like to do school work. I hate doing school work because you get used to not doing it after a couple of years, and it's really hard to go back. But I think when I have a steady place to stay, I feel like I could do whatever I want. I won't have a mother telling me what to do. I won't have anyone telling me what to do.

My mom said to me, "I don't care where you live or what you do, as long as you're happy, as long as it's right for you." And she knows what's right for me.

I want to do something with myself, I want to go back to school for a couple of years. I'm not talking about no nine-year college diploma, you know, masters degree. I'll take it slow, one step at a time. We'll see, you know? First of all, I don't have the money for that, but I still want to go to some college in the next year.

I could never go back to Berkeley High. I feel like I've outgrown everyone in the whole school. I couldn't deal with all those kids all around. I'm a kid, too, I'm as old as them.

Maybe I'll go to a community college, take it slow, a few classes at a time. I'll probably have to take some basic courses, English, math, and stuff. After that I don't know. Maybe some music or something, or maybe psychology or something. I don't like computers, I never did.

I'll take it one step at a time.

There are some people in the park, people who have dropped out, who got straight A's. And they regret it. A lot of them are trying to go back, but somehow this park always drags you back. It's not like it's going to kill you. It's just that you have to be strong.

I'm trying to work it out with my mother. I haven't talked to my father for a long time. But I know one thing about my family. They'll always love me. For a while, I didn't appreciate it. Everyone was telling me, don't treat your mother like that. Whenever I want to go back, she'll be there. That's one thing.

I try to do things for her now. I really appreciate it. I've been so confused, but I know that I'm still the same person. I'm still living. So, we'll make it. Somehow.

The Dropout

I am an eternity of myself.
But I change myself
Even if I don't know who I am.
Can somebody tell me? No?
I have to find out
Who I am. I am a mystery.

—PAULA LITSHAUER-TISCHLER, 11

Sara, 15

"The young, gifted, middle class and bored. Fits me well."

The Dropout

I'm a dropout, yeah. I'm only fifteen, so I haven't acutally dropped out yet, but I don't go to school.

I quit school before I even started it. I'm just doing it technically now, but when I was in grammar school, it was the same thing. I wasn't really going to school. I was there in body but I wasn't paying attention. I wasn't doing the work, nothing. Now, I'm just doing the same thing, just technically and really and finally. I don't think about school. I just don't go to it. It wasn't a decision. The decision would be to go to it.

It doesn't make sense. That's what everybody says. Of course it doesn't make sense. How could it possibly make sense? I mean, if you're looking for why we're dropping out to make sense, forget it. It doesn't make sense.

The young, gifted, middle class and bored. Fits me well.

So why do we do it? I don't know why we do it, we just do. Because we're not going to go to class! There's different reasons for every time that I don't go to every class. I mean, there's one day I won't go because of what we'll be discussing, or the book we're reading in English, I'll have already finished.

The fact is there's just no way I'm going to start going to class and being a scholar. Like you're not going to be a tap dancer, as far as you know, right? Well, I'm not going to be a scholar. I could be, but I'm not going to try.

It's boring but that's not the only reason. I mean, 'cause sometimes when you're cutting, you're bored. But at least you're not stuck there being bored. You can go somewhere else and be not bored. I'm not stuck in class because I don't go to class. Or when I do go to class and I feel stuck in class, I leave class. But if I wanted to be a scholar and tried to be a scholar, I wouldn't do that. I don't subject myself to something that I don't like.

How do the teachers react? I don't stop and ask, you know, on my way out of the class, "By the way, how do you feel?" I mean, I assume that they either resent it or are insulted or it's a relief. But I think that if I'm leaving a class I'm resenting something or insulting and could care less about how the teacher thinks of me.

I never talked to teachers about kids that drop out. Sometimes, it's a sad thing. I mean, if you talked to any of my teachers they'd go, "Oh, how sad Sara dropped out." But, you know, sometimes there are some teachers who will look at it the way I do, which is, "She's just not doing it, so why should she stay in and make my life difficult?"

My sister, okay, is just like the same thing. She dropped out. And she lives with my other sister, who went to high school, went through college, a straight-A student. She's in real estate now. My two sisters, the dropout and the success, live in the same place and wear the same clothes, okay. So I don't see the point. I mean they're at the same level with total opposite ends of education. So I'd rather take my younger sister's way out, thank you.

I'm trying to figure out new footsteps of my own. If I go to school and go to college, I'll follow in my mother's footsteps. And if I don't go to school but stay in Berkeley, I'll be following in my sister's footsteps.

When I started drugs in the ninth grade, I started cutting. I don't know if I would have not cut if I'd not done drugs. But since I do do drugs and I do cut, I have no idea whether it's got anything to do with it. I don't think so.

They've offered me the alternative of juvenile court, you know, and foster home. That's interesting, by the way, because the guy from SART, the Student Attendance Review Team, called me and my mother and said, "Yes, within thirty days if you don't start going to class, we're going to send you to a foster home." And it's already been much longer than thirty days.

There's nothing they can do. Once they tried to get my mother's boyfriend to go to all my classes with me. I was heavily amused. He couldn't take it longer than four weeks. He dropped out after four weeks. That's proving my point. Because even while he was going to all my classes, when we went swimming, which was third period, he would drop me off and go get a cappucino, okay? He left after four weeks. Something about it's too boring, and there's no reason why I should do this.

I was offered a chance to go to Maybeck. Maybeck is a private school. I didn't want to go because I like the people I saw at Berkeley High. Then my mother made me go and take the test. I went, and people said, "We love you, come on." And then I went home and said, "Yeah, well, I'm in." And my mother said, "Well, I don't want you to go to Maybeck." I didn't bother to ask her about it because I decided at that point that my mother was cracked, since she had been the one to insist on me going. I think my mother is insane. And I don't think she's insane because she's my mother. I just think that the woman is cracked.

We fight a lot . . . about school and how irresponsible I am and how I'm a failure. I enjoy it. I love it 'cause I always win. I'm cracked too.

What I do all day depends on the day and what there is to do. I might go to the library, I might go to a different class. I might just walk around and meditate. Usually I just sit in pottery all day until it's dance class and then I go to dance and then I go to pottery.

It's not teachers' attitude. There's nothing they can do. I mean, with thirty-five students in a class, how is a teacher going to notice whether a couple of the students are in all of their classes? There's nothing the school can do about it.

The Dropout

I know I'm screwing myself up, but I only know I'm screwing myself up because everybody's told me that I'm screwing myself up. And since so many people have told me the exact same thing, you know, that it doesn't make sense, that I'm shooting myself in the foot, I believe them. But not really. I mean, 'cause if twenty-five percent of the kids drop out, as you say, then something must happen to them, you know? And I want to find out what.

I wasn't ever a scholar. I never did anything, so everybody always said, you know, when I got remarks on my report cards instead of grades: "She's brilliant, but she doesn't do the work. She doesn't do her homework. She doesn't pay attention in class. But she's so bright. Oh my God, what are we going to do?"

When I started dropping out, I was living with my stepfather and my mother and her boyfriend were living in the back house. I rarely saw my mother.

My mother went to Catholic school. She went to St. Mary's. She's a Ph.D., you know, works at home doing freelance editing. She's Miss Brilliant. She thinks that she's a success. I think that what she has I could easily live without. She's stuck where she is. I mean, she's got this house and she's got a mortgage on it, blah blah blah. Which is exactly not what I want, okay?

And my stepfather is not the most responsible person in the world. He's got a job, he went to college, but he's got this really light attitude about life, which is understandable since he makes $60,000 a year. But I don't really care if I have enough money to live, I just want to be enjoying myself, if that makes sense.

A while ago I got a little insulted that my father hadn't contacted me at all since I was three. You know, and I walked around for about a day going, "Well, he decided when I was three, that I was a failure." Then I thought, why do I care? I can be depressed about all these things. I can boo-hoo and wail and cry and sob about how my mother never paid any attention to me and all this stuff, but it's not how I look at it.

How do I look at it? I don't, I don't. We're all going to die anyway. And that's the only thing there is to be serious about, that everybody's going to die. I mean, you're going to grow up and I'm going to be a bum on the streets, but we're both going to look the same as skeletons. So why should I care what happens to me in the meantime?

If people are going to classify me, they might as well do it as a dropout. What bothers me is being classified at all. But it doesn't matter what I'm classified as.

I see myself as a pretty flighty fifteen-year-old. I don't know. I see myself as different at different times. Right now, I see a silly fifteen-year-old who doesn't really know what's going on. I don't know. I don't look at myself, I look at other people. I understand and realize that if I want to do anything I like I should go to school and, say, yeah, I've got to go to school, I've got to do this and this and this. I'm not going to do it.

The Dropout

It's like quitting smoking. You know you need to and you say you're going to, but you don't. I sort of skip the step of saying I'm going to. Since I'm not going to, I don't. And I say no, I'm not going to. Everybody always used to say, "Will you go to school this semester? Will you go to school today?" And I'd always say, "Yes, yes, yes. I'll change, I'll be wonderful." No. No, I won't.

What do I see? I don't see anything. I don't look for anything.

It's weird, but I don't know what's going to happen to me. And I don't know whether I'm going to be some old decrepit disgusting bum on the streets, but I know I have enough of a handle on myself that I know that I can make myself happy no matter what. And I will enjoy, or at least be interested in whatever goes on.

I would not mind being a freelance editor if I could quit at any time. It's just not my idea of the ideal lifestyle.

What's my ideal? Well, there's this editor, food editor, named Calvin Trillin, who works for *The New Yorker*, I think, and he's written a few books. And apparently what he does is just travels around and eats. Yeah! He and his wife live in New York , and they travel all over the place and eat. And I guess that's just what he does for a living, is eat.

I can travel and eat. I can learn to type or something and do little odd jobs. All you need to do to travel is have the money to go to the place. And the money for an apartment, which is first month, last money, damages, and if you can talk it helps a whole lot. And I'm sure I can do that, you know. It doesn't take a whole lot.

I don't gloat about the fact that I'm a dropout, I gloat about the fact that I'm me. I like Sara. I think Sara's a great person and so whatever it is that I do, I condone. I mean, to myself. I'll say this is terrible and this is awful and I won't expect anybody else to condone it, but I'm still saying, "Hey, I did it, so that's not so bad." Why should I feel ashamed of myself. If I feel ashamed of myself I should just commit suicide and be done with it. And as long as I'm still having fun being alive then I'm going to have fun being alive. And that does not mean going off and being some self-martyr and being ashamed of myself. I'm not ashamed of nobody else and I'm not going to start with me.

Am I going back to school? Absolutely not. Well, I mean, that's like saying I'm going to die when I'm thirty. I can't definitely say I'm not going to go back to school, but I can't possibly imagine why I would want to.

What I'm learning when I go to school, I can learn faster by reading the books that my mother's got lining our walls, which I do.

What is my opinion of education? Do you mean education as Plato saw it or as I see it? I see it as learning and it doesn't matter how you do it as long as you learn something.

The Dropout

41

Allons! the road is before us!
It is safe—I have tried it—my own feet have tried it well—
be not detained!

Let the paper remain on the desk unwritten, and the book
on the shelf unopened!
Let the tools remain in the workshop! let the money remain
unearned!
Let the school stand! mind not the cry of the teacher!
Let the preacher preach in his pulpit! let the lawyer plead in
the court, and the judge expound the law.
Comerado, I give you my hand!

—"Song of the Open Road"
WALT WHITMAN

Mario, 16

C.E.: Do you want to accomplish anything?

Mario: Me?

C.E.: Yeah.

Mario: Yeah.

C.E.: What?

Mario: Be something.

CE: Where were you born?

MARIO: Newark, New Jersey.

CE: And you lived here your whole life?

MARIO: Yeah.

CE: Who do you live with?

MARIO: My mother and my father, and a brother and a sister.

CE: How old and what grade were you in when you dropped out?

MARIO: Sixteen. Ninth grade.

CE: Why did you drop out?

MARIO: Basically, it was the fact that I was behind. It wasn't my fault.

CE: Whose fault was it?

MARIO: It was actually the fault of the last school I went to.

CE: Why was it their fault?

MARIO: Because I was there for my freshman year, two years ago, and I had gone through the whole year. I had a C average. Towards the end of the year I was going to leave the school. I was going to transfer. When my father went to transfer me, they didn't want me to leave. My father did want me to leave so we went through the paperwork. They sent a copy of my transcripts, like what I had done. It wasn't it.

CE: What was it?

MARIO: I don't know.

CE: So how did your parents react?

MARIO: Not too good, because now what I'm trying to do is I'm trying to take a GED.

CE: So you just decided on your own, because you were going to be held back a year?

MARIO: Yeah.

CE: So, did you just decide on your own, I refuse to do that?

MARIO: Yeah, more or less.

CE: You said, "I'm going to quit"?

MARIO: Yeah.

CE: Did you discuss it with anyone?

MARIO: Yeah.

CE: Like who?

MARIO: My father. And I went to see a counselor and I talked with my mother about it.

The Dropout

CE: Did anyone try to persuade you to stay in school?

MARIO: Yeah. A lot of people.

CE: Who?

MARIO: Aside from my family, friends.

CE: Did they have any effect at all?

MARIO: No.

CE: Before you dropped out, how often did you miss school or cut class?

MARIO: Before I dropped out? The last school I went to I started there the last few days of September and I cut the first week I was there.

     Second week I went for two days. The third week I cut the whole week. I told my mother and we went into the school and we just talked about it—why I was doing this. And so I was just transferred out.

CE: Were you ever suspended?

MARIO: No.

CE: Did you fight?

MARIO: No.

CE: That's not a problem.

MARIO: No.

CE: Did you like school?

MARIO: Yeah, more or less.

CE: What was the less part?

MARIO: Like the long classes. Doin' the homework.

CE: What didn't you like about it?

MARIO: The classes were too long. Like on hot days you have to sit in a classroom with thirty, forty people, and this kind of strong odor comes out of there after a while.

CE: What would you have rather done?

MARIO: You might say that you like something, but when you really look at it, there's something that you don't like about it. I liked it, but I didn't like it. But I shoulda' stayed there.

CE: You're planning on going back?

MARIO: I want to take the GED.

CE: What were your teachers like?

MARIO: They were okay.

The Dropout

47

CE: Did you respect them?
MARIO: Yeah. At least I let them think I did. But really I did.

CE: You really didn't?
MARIO: No, really I did.

CE: Did they respect you?
MARIO: Yes.

CE: So, all right, what are you doing now?
MARIO: Just hangin' out.

CE: Have you tried to get a job?
MARIO: Yeah.

CE: And?
Mario: Nothin'

CE: They're just not hiring?
MARIO: No. Well, they're hiring, but they're not hiring me.

CE: Why is that?
MARIO: Probably because I have like no experience or nothin' or I'm not of age or I'm not in school. They take all these things into account.

CE: How old do you have to be to take a GED?
MARIO: Sixteen with a waiver.

CE: And do you think you can pass the GED?
MARIO: Yeah.

CE: And then what?
MARIO: I want to take some courses at Essex County.

CE: What would you like to be doing five years from now?
MARIO: I'm not sure.

CE: Did you ever think of college?
MARIO: Yeah.

CE: Do you regret what you did, dropping out?
MARIO: In some respects, yeah.

CE: In what way?
MARIO: I think if I woulda' stayed there, like I coulda' done this and then that and I coulda' had this and woulda' done a few things and if I, like stayed out, I won't be able to do things that I wanted to do.

CE: Like what?

MARIO: Like just being with people and like being back, like the prom and things like that in the high school.

CE: How does it make you feel to be called a dropout?

MARIO: Not too good.

CE: Why not?

MARIO: It's like another word for bum.

CE: Is that how you think of yourself? Do you think you're a bum?

MARIO: Yeah, more or less.

CE: What does your family think?

MARIO: I'm not sure.

CE: Do you think that dropping out is an answer?

MARIO: No.

CE: You don't think you could go back, though?

MARIO: I could if I wanted to, but I don't want to go back.

CE: Why not?

MARIO: Well, I'd still be behind.

CE: What do you think is the reason you dropped out? Do you think the problem is with the schools or with people's home lives, or . . . where is it?

MARIO: With me, somewhere.

CE: What could be changed? What can people do? There are people who really want to know what they could change that would make a difference for kids to stay in school.

MARIO: What they can change?

CE: Yeah. What would have made a difference for you?

MARIO: If I wouldna' failed that first year.

CE: And could they have done something to keep that from happening?

MARIO: Yeah.

CE: What?

MARIO: I didn't fail on my own. Like I said, I had a C average and I don't think that that's a failing average.

CE: So what happened?

MARIO: I don't know.

CE: Would more tutoring have helped or more special attention?

MARIO: No, not really.

CE: Could the school have done anything, aside from passing you? Was it their fault or was it your fault?

MARIO: I don't feel like I did anything that would have made me repeat the year. I didn't get into any trouble with people. Once in a while I would do something like I'd have to stay after school, but that was it.

CE: You get a lot of shit from your family about this?

MARIO: Well, yeah.

CE: And you just ignore it, or . . .

MARIO: Yeah.

CE: Is that hard to live with? Is it hard to live at home with that pressure?

MARIO: Yeah.

CE: Are you happy with what you do?

MARIO: Sometimes, yeah.

CE: Tell me about your days.

MARIO: Days? Sometimes I just get up in the morning.

CE: Like what time?

MARIO: About 7:30. I go out . . .

CE: With other kids? Do you hang out with a lot of other kids who have also left school?

MARIO: No. They just cut for the day.

CE: So do you hang out near a school?

MARIO: Sometimes, yeah.

CE: What do you do?

MARIO: Do all kinds of things . . . (chuckle)

CE: You just hang out.

MARIO: Yeah.

CE: Is money important to you?

MARIO: No, not really.

CE: No?

MARIO: No.

CE: What was important to you? What is important to you? What are things you value most, care about most?

MARIO: My family. I mean, material things? Anything? My family.

CE: Do you feel like you have a good communication with your family?

MARIO: Yeah. Yeah.

CE: So it must be hard to have them be so important and be doing something that they obviously don't approve of.

MARIO: Yeah.

CE: What do you say to them?

MARIO: I don't say nothin'.

CE: What do you do? How do you live with it?

MARIO: I just like to try not to listen when they start talking about it.

CE: How do you do that?

MARIO: If they're like in the kitchen talkin about it, I leave the kitchen.

CE: How do you think other people describe you?

MARIO: Other people? I don't know. Some people might say, well, I know some people who will say, well, he finally did a smart thing, he dropped out. And other people say that's stupid.

CE: Who says it's stupid and who says it's not?

MARIO: Like, friends. Like I have two categories of friends: ones that all agree with what I'm doing, others who disagree with what I'm doing. And the ones who agree are the ones who are doin' the same thing.

CE: Friends of yours have dropped out as well?

MARIO: Yeah.

CE: Did you think of yourself as a dropout?

MARIO: Yes.

CE: Does that feel like a negative word to you?

MARIO: Yeah.

CE: What would your ideal job be?

MARIO: I couldn't tell. Like for the rest of my life?

CE: Yeah.

MARIO: Nothing that I could get right now.

CE: What would it be?

MARIO: What would it be? Not sure.

CE: If somebody came up to you and said, Mario, you can do anything you want. I'll see to it that you get into any school you want to go to . . .

MARIO: Oh . . . huh huh.

CE: Give you as much money as you need to get through school . . .

MARIO: Engineering.

CE: Engineering? You think you could do that?
MARIO: Yeah.

CE: What keeps you from trying?
MARIO: Probably me.

CE: Can you think of anything else? Did we forget to ask you anything?
MARIO: No.

CE: Anything you want to say? You think a book like this can help?
MARIO: Some people probably, but some people can't be helped.

CE: Why? You know kids like that?
MARIO: Yeah.

CE: They've just never been to school?
MARIO: They quit the third grade.

CE: And you don't think there's anything that can be done . . .
MARIO: For them? No hope. I mean, if they wanted to, you know, you might accomplish
           something. But they don't want to, so they not gonna get nothin'.

CE: Do you want to accomplish anything?
MARIO: Me?

CE: Yeah.
MARIO: Yeah.

CE: What?
MARIO: Be something.

CE: Does it ever feel like you're choosing the hard way to do it?
MARIO: If I wanted to, I could. It'd be real easy for me. I could make really good money.
           but I don't want to.

CE: Why? Like what? Getting caught, or . . .
MARIO: Yeah, getting caught. I know too many people with all their problems.

CE: Is that the biggest force, once you get into school?
MARIO: Mmm-hmm.

CE: Drugs?
MARIO: Mmm-hmm.

CE: If you had a little brother, what would you tell him?
MARIO: Tell him not to hang out with me.

CE: I guess that's it, unless you got anything else to say.
MARIO: Uh-uh.

The Dropout

Purgatory is a place
between heaven and hell.
It's not good and it's
not bad. It's sort of
like here, where we are now.

—DENESE, 12

Juliet, 16

"I'd give anything to have a home
And a mom who really cared about me."

The Dropout

I'm an only child. I never met my real father. He was a sailor, Irish. His name was Skipper Cuddy. One day I'd like to meet him. My mother has been in and out of jail three-quarters of my life.

I was two years old when my mom got arrested for smuggling cocaine across the Mexican border. She went to jail there, so I didn't really know my mom until I was seven. We moved to San Francisco. Half a year later she got married. Her new husband adopted me. He had two children, so they became my step-brother and step-sister. They were all very supportive, and they really wanted to go to school. So I went to school in San Francisco, to junior high.

My mom and I did not get along. We did not know each other very well. We fought a lot. We were a lot alike, so we were very aggravated with each other. Plus, I was mad at her for leaving me my whole child life. I was mad at her that I didn't know her. Now I look back at it and I feel bad, but I was mad then. I was angry because I thought it was unfair that I didn't know my mom through my childhood.

I lived with her from about seven to twelve. My mom used to beat me. It started with a slap, a hard slap. It ended with belts, my stepfather's. She never did it when he was home. But when he wasn't coming home, when they fought or whatever, or weren't getting along, I used to get beat. For little things, like losing my house keys.

I took it for about a year and a half, two years. One day, around two years ago, when I got as tall as my mother, she was going to hit me. She pulled her hand back and she went to slap me. I just remember feeling the tension in my hand. That was the first time I remember ever feeling juiced, you know how you say it?

I just felt this tension in my head. At first I felt it in my brain. And then I felt it throughout my body. I felt it in my hands. This tension went up me, and I just hit her. Like that. Right in her face. I caught her first because her hand was way back and I was already up here, in her face. I hit her as hard as I could.

I felt so bad. But I felt like, there, now do you know how it feels?

My mom would always cry and say, "I'm sorry, I won't do it again. I don't know why I did it. I'm sorry, you just made me angry." Or this or that. Whatever. And I would accept it. But then it would happen again. I just got tired. I really got tired.

That was the last time for a long time. The second time it happened, I left.

I was thirteen. I ran away from home and that's just a long, crazy story. I lived in abandoned buildings, which we call squats, for over a year. I was very, very into punk.

The Dropout

I had no hair, no eyebrows, combat boots, a leather jacket. I would smoke anything I could. What I wanted was to be rebellious. I took one of the paths that I knew would annoy, would bother my parents. I was so angry, so upset. More, I was just sad. But it just came into anger, because I felt that nobody could understand me.

I lived in an abandoned building down on Market Street in San Francisco—the worst possible neighborhood—climbing through broken glass windows. I walked around with a metal pipe because my friends had been beat up and raped and, you know, men and shit, you know?

In a way it makes you strong, and in a way I can't even come to the reality that I've been through. I hide it in my day-to-day life. I never really talk about it. I been through so much, just so much. I've eaten in churches and all those places.

I had no money. I would wear whatever I could. When I first left home I was about one hundred and forty pounds. I got down to a hundred and ten pounds. I was very into drugs, very sick. Disease and shit, you know from nasty people. When you're living in the street and drinking and getting high and not eating, and wasting your life away, food is not really important. Except for when you get really hungry. It seems like other things are more important.

Then I got arrested in San Francisco on Broadway, which is a very nasty street, for fighting drunk. I don't even remember what happened. I was in a juvenile hall lock-up in San Francisco for two and a half months.

I had nowhere to turn. All my friends were on the outside. I was locked up. I just couldn't deal with it. I felt very suicidal at the time. I thought suicide was an easy way out.

Later, when I was fifteen I cut my wrists and freaked out and then cried, and realized that wasn't what I wanted. But that was later. If you try to kill yourself in juvenile hall they'll send you to a psychiatric ward, you know? No matter how desperate you're feeling, how lonely you're feeling. I wasn't even really feeling I wanted to kill myself. I just wanted a way out. I just wanted a way to be myself, to apologize to my parents, to start living my life again. Now I look back and think, God, girl, you're crazy.

I had three choices. Suicide. Going to a boarding home in Ohio. Or to a friend of my mother's who had come to the jail, a lady that I knew that had managed my mom's clothing shop. She owned a store at the time. And she asked me if I would come and stay in Hawaii with her, in Maui. So I could get my shit together, and I could go to school and just be myself. I thought, I'm either going to go or stay in juvenile hall and end up killing myself. I just felt so lonely. I felt like I had nowhere to turn.

The Dropout

Anyway, I decided to go to Hawaii. It was a fresh start. It was beautiful. I had a good time. I went to Maui High School. This was the beginning of the ninth grade. I went the first three months of school in the ninth grade. I was doing okay. Then I started meeting people, Hawaiian people, Asians, Filipinos. I started finding out where to hang out, where all the parties were, where all the kegs were. I started going into the jungle and picking mushrooms, magic mushrooms in the fields. You pick them to make milkshakes and trip, like acid.

I wasn't really into drugs. I don't drink. I don't shoot up or anything. I never did. My main thing is marijuana. I've always liked marijuana because it doesn't make me crazy. It just makes me feel mellow and good. And I like to trip on things. But I think when I moved to Hawaii, that made it worse because there was just so much weed out there. I can actually blame that. It's part of the reason I stopped going to school. I just started partying. That was ninth and tenth grades.

In the middle of the tenth, I was still not in school. I was staying in a group home because the lady I was living with—my mom's friend—found out I wasn't going to school and lying to her about it. I lied to her because I was scared that she was going to be ashamed of me. I was scared that what did happen would happen. We started fighting, and it was just like another fucking trip, another trip living with my mom, you know? So I ended up staying in a group home.

Then, about the middle of the tenth grade, I got a phone call from my step-sister in San Francisco. My step-sister said, "Juliet, I don't know what has happened." There were cops raiding our house and tearing everything apart, she said. My mom and dad were not there. They had been taken away in handcuffs, with news cameras and everything, she said. She didn't know why. It was on the first page of *The San Francisco Chronicle*.

They were in jail because supposedly they were making and selling twenty percent of America's LSD. Selling it and producing, bagging it and sending it all over the world. Not just a couple of countries, all over the world.

I don't know anything about this. I really don't. I can't tell you if it's true. I can't tell you if they were set up. I don't know. I tend to think that it's true, but I tend to think that they—how do you say, when they make something bigger out of it—exaggerate it. Maybe they had sold a little bit of acid to some friends or something. Both my parents were hippies, total straight-up hippies in the sixties. Lived in a school bus with long hair, you know? That's what it said in the newspapers. That's what it said in *The Chronicle*.

My parents are gone now. I can see them. Yes, I can visit with them. But I'll never be able to call my mom, not for ten and a half years. I had a family, I didn't get along with my mom. I took it all for granted.

The Dropout

But I never really regret that part of my life. Sometimes I'll see girls these days who want to be like me, who want to be really punk, who want to run away from home and do all this stuff. Sometimes I feel like shaking them because I'm so angry. If I could get a hold of them and explain what I've been through, how it's not trendy, and it's not fun to run away from home and have to live with pants that are holey and be cold and sleep anywhere you can, and get high and go to places and trash and things. It's just not the way to live.

Now I'm getting my life together. I've met a man who has made me happier than I have been in a long time. I'm four months pregnant. It's scary, but I want it. We're very young. He's seventeen and I'm sixteen. All my life I've always wanted a baby.

I can't really say that the pregnancy was planned. If I told you that it was planned, it would be a lie. But I feel like, you know, like this is right for me.

I've had an abortion before. The first time I ever made love I got pregnant. It was two days after my thirteenth birthday. I was only having periods for six months before that. The guy I had an abortion from the first time overdosed and died.

My boyfriend is from Mexico. I've been with him for five months. We're about to make six months on the sixteenth of this month. That's also a very short time, but there's some connection. You know? I feel like I could be happy with him for the rest of my life. He's an illegal alien. He's a sweetheart. Both his parents are in Mexico. He stays with his auntie. He's very moody, a Cancer. Sometimes he's an asshole. Sometimes he can be the worst asshole. It's like there's two sides of him. Sometimes I don't know who he is.

After I have my baby, I plan to be with my baby for a year, a year and a half, to raise my baby. The beginning is real important time. And then I'll have somebody like Sharon be the godmother of my baby.

He's planning to take care of the baby, he's all for it. He's pretty much supportive. I mean, he doesn't ever say anything bad about it. When he found out that I was pregnant, he was more happy than I was. I mean, I was happy but I just felt like I wasn't really ready.

We've talked about marriage, but it's not something that we really sit hard and think about. We're both young, and we both have so many things that we want to do with our lives.

My mom was very upset when I told her I was pregnant. I couldn't take it. I had talked to her once before—she only called every so often—before I had known. I wanted to tell her so bad, I just felt like I needed to tell her, even though she was far away. I felt that was better, to tell her when she was far away, so that I wouldn't have to see, you know, her face. I could just have it be, Mom, this is what's happening.

The Dropout

She was very upset because she messed up my life. She didn't say that that's why, but I know that that's why, because she feels guilty. Anybody in their right mind who got arrested when they had a baby two years old, and didn't see the baby until the baby was seven, would feel bad. And the baby will probably feel bad too because they would feel that that was unfair.

I'm angry at her, but I can't be angry because everybody messes up. I wonder why she needed the money. I wonder if it was an addiction, the drugs, or I wonder if she just needed the money. I don't know. Some day I'm going to sit down with a tape recorder and I'm going to ask her all these questions. Or I'm going to spill my guts out to her on a recorder and just ask her why she did everything. Why?

Right now I'm at this point where I'm just laggering. I haven't been to school in three years. I'm getting to the point where I want to start going to school. I want to get a job. Just yesterday I went down to the welfare office and stood in line and filled out lots of applications, and I'm going to get welfare.

I'm starting to be with girlfriends more. Most times I stay with my friend Sharon. Me and her became really good friends. She started going out with her boyfriend Tommy around the same time I started going out with Jose.

And I met another girl, Anita. I hang around with her, or just talk to her sometimes. Even though we aren't like the best of friends, I needed somebody. I needed a friend who was a woman, a girl around the same age as me. No matter if you have your boyfriend, if you have your baby, or if you just have your mom and dad, you still need friends. Teenage girls need to have teenage friends, teenage girlfriends.

I didn't go to school last year at Berkeley High School because I didn't know anybody. I felt uncomfortable, and I wasn't ready to go and meet friends. I felt like I was going through way too much shit. Right now, I'm supposed to be a junior there. I just didn't go to the first day, didn't go the second day. I didn't want to come up and walk into a classroom with new people. Especially walking in in the middle of the year. It's embarrassing.

But I'm going to go back to school. After I have my baby, I'm going to get somebody to take care of it. Get some kind of education. And if I just can't deal with school, I'm going to get a GED and then go to college, learn to do something, get into something that would be like fashion design or art or something.

School was never a major priority in my life. My parents always pushed toward it. I think maybe if they hadn't pushed so hard, maybe I wouldn't have gone over. They didn't push me that hard. It's just that if they had given me a little more choice, a little more freedom, not like, get out and go to school and this and that, you know?

The Dropout

I'm trying hard now to get myself together. I'm waiting a little while. I plan to go up to Garberville, near Oregon. I have some friends up there. They had two big, huge Newfoundland dogs, a hundred and seventy pounds each. They're like humongous teddy bears. I miss them dearly.

Anyway, I just plan to get my stuff together. I plan to wait a little while. I don't want to do anything too stressful because of the pregnancy. I just need a roof over my head so I can mellow for a while, get my stuff together. Get my stuff together financially. Mentally, too.

I look at my friends who have a place to live, have a beautiful home, have parents who care about them. I'll go to my friends' houses and they'll fight over things that are so petty to me because, right now, both my parents are in jail. I'll look at them and I'll just feel like it isn't fair, because I'd give anything to have a home and a mom who really cared about me.

If you have parents who care about you, that's your blood no matter what they do to you. If you have a home, if you have a good home, even a place where you can go and keep your stuff and eat with your family and talk with your family, and get loved and give love—just take care of it, just nurture it, because when it's not there, you'll realize what you had.

The Dropout

Do you hear the children weeping, oh my brothers . . . ?
They are weeping bitterly
They are weeping in the playtime of the others,
In the country of the free.

—"The Cry of the Children"
ELIZABETH BARRETT BROWNING

Part Two

The Runaways

M

ira, a seventeen-year-old runaway, lives on the streets of Minneapolis. Julie Horowitz met her at a dinner for homeless youth at St. Mark's Church. They talked while she ate, and afterwards, sitting on a lawn, Mira continued talking spontaneously for hours.

Someone passing on the sidewalk would have suspected nothing unusual. From a distance, Mira appears like many teenagers, slightly unkempt, wearing torn shorts, a badly worn t-shirt and a black leather jacket. She wore no jewelry and used no makeup. In contrast to the stories she told, she had an aura of innocence.

Closer, one sees the broken blood vessel under an eye of her pleasant, small-featured face. It was but one of her permanent scars, the result, she said, of the numerous beatings she has received from her father and step-mother all her life. She pushed up her sleeve and revealed a fresh bruise, a souvenir of her latest stay at home.

She ran away from home and dropped out of school to flee the abuse, she said. She lived in foster homes, group homes, shelters, occasionally returning or, against her will, being returned to her parents' home. When asked why, Mira turned the palms of her hands upward and said, "Don't you understand? The system is screwed! The system is screwed!"

Mira has taken refuge from her parents and the system in a life of pure uncertainty on the streets. The price is often hunger, discomfort, illicit sex, and unhappiness.

Months later, the memory of Mira remained vivid and unshakeable. Julie Horowitz wrote of her, "Nowhere was she happy. Nowhere did she receive the love, understanding, and respect that she desires and deserves. Hers may appear to be an isolated, extreme, offbeat case, but it isn't. Her problems are connected to the mainstream. All these problems tie together. We cannot address hunger without addressing education. We cannot address health without addressing homelessness."

Thelma Foster met the other two runaways, Linda and Odetta, at the Port Authority Bus Terminal in New York City. The project director of the Youth Services Unit of the Port Authority agreed to let her interview runaways that staff workers picked up, if they consented. When they pick up people who look as if they're lost or have no place to go, they bring them into an office, phone their parents, have a social worker intervene.

At first, they were hostile and wary. Unlike Mira, they were extremely cautious about what they said. That's how their lives have instructed them.

The Runaways

66

These two runaways probably went home, but they probably didn't stay very long. Thelma wrote later, "It was really, really sad, because they were asking for so little. They should be getting a mile, but they can't even get an inch."

She saw them as incredibly strong people: "They're probably not going to be successful in a worldly sense, in the American sense of material wealth. They don't have the academic background, the clout or the contacts. Who knows if they'll ever get out of the economic straits they're in. But those girls have something difficult to describe or put your finger on. They've got the ability to really give something. I fell in love with them immediately. I felt so linked to them, because they just opened up like flowers on a sunny day."

Teen Editors: *Julie Horowitz*
Thelma Foster

Mira, 17

"Screw that, you send me home,
I'll just run. I'm not going home
to get my ass kicked every day again."

The Runaways

I used to go to school just to get out of the house. I failed all my classes, not because I'm dumb or anything, but because I didn't care about school. It was boring for me. I knew everything there was to know already. The only thing I went to school for was to see my freinds and to get away from my parents. My parents and I have a very bad relationship. I knew somewhere soon I'd end up getting kicked out of my house again.

The first time I was kicked out was in the middle of March. When they told me I had to leave, I had no place to go. Then a friend of the family called up and asked my mom what was going on. She and my mom are empathic.

My mom said, "Yeah, Mira's leaving and she doesn't have anyplace to stay. I'm worried about her. She might get killed or something while she's out there."

My parents didn't know that after being in a group home for seven months and living in South Minneapolis, I know basically everything there is to know about South Minneapolis and the uptown area. Cops know me, and they don't say nothing. They don't even bother. They've tried to crack me doing a lot of things, and I've always gotten off. I'm really lucky.

I was court-ordered to a group home called Home Away. They tried to pick me up for being a runaway, but considering they never knew where I hung around, it was impossible for them to catch me.

The only thing I ever did wrong was run away from a group home. I didn't ever want to go home again. As far as I was concerned I was never going home. You had to be there four weeks before you got a pass home. When I went home on my first pass, I thought maybe things would have changed in the four weeks I was gone. They hadn't, so when I got back to the group home, I split.

The first time I ran away from home was April third last year. I had turned my step-mom in for punching me in the face. They sent me into a foster home. They were telling me I was never going to go home again. This is why I say the system is screwed. They said I wasn't ever going to have to go home again and then, it was May second, they told me I was going home.

I said, "Screw that. You send me home, I'll just run. I'm not going home to get my ass kicked every day again."

They didn't believe me. They sent me home and I ran away.

Basically, everybody's out on the streets because they don't get along with their parents, or what happens is the same thing that happened to me. You get into a fight with your parents and end up getting your ass kicked. When my parents did that to me, I reported them. I ended up in foster homes and the treatment facility, and they always sent me back home. The system is really screwed.

I've got a permanently busted blood vessel in my right eye because I got punched in that eye twice within three months. The first time my dad did that to me, I ended up with three lumps on the left side of my head, five on the right side, a huge black eye. Three months later, my step-mom punched me in the right eye.

I turned my parents in again, so they sent me to the second foster home. At the time I was real naive about the streets and all that crap. I was scared to death. I thought I was going to be stuck in a group home with female murderers. You know, I'd ask, "What are you in here for?"

"Oh, I'm in here for robbing a bank," I imagined one would say.

"I'm in here for murder," another would say.

Then they'd ask me, and I'd have to look down at the ground and say, "Running away." You know, big crime.

So I went home from June through July. Sometime around July fifteenth, my dad gave me the alternative, "Leave now or listen to your step-mom." She and I haven't gotten along for seven years. (I keep saying seven years. I said seven years three years ago, so it's about ten years that we haven't gotten along.)

He said, "You can leave now, call Bill, or grow up and do what Mell tells you." Bill is my social worker.

"There's no way I can grow up and accept Mell as my mother," I said.

I remember too many years where there was nobody there except for me, Teresa, and my Dad. Teresa's my 16-year-old sister. She still lives at home. Me and Teresa's the only full-blooded sisters. Angela's gonna be ten, Danny just turned eight, Connie just turned five, and Jennifer just turned two. Angela through Jennifer are my step-mom's kids. I know if I were to have grown up thinking that Mell was actually my mother, it would've been a different story. But I know she wasn't because I remember times of being alone.

My real mother left my dad when I was two. Until then, she used to go out nights. My dad used to work nights. Half an hour after he'd leave, she'd leave. Half an hour before he came home, she came home. The whole time, the seven hours she was gone, I'd be laying on the middle of our living room floor. I was a baby, still wearing diapers. There'd be a piss stain eight inches in diameter where I'd been left on the floor all night. My dad always knew but he never said anything to her because he didn't want her to leave him, because he was seriously in love with her. Finally, one day, she up and left him. I have never seen her since.

Any rate, in answer to my dad's ultimatum, I said, "Fine, I'll leave."

My dad said, "No, you're not leaving. You wait. We'll call Bill on Monday."

We called, and he set up a court date. I ended up going to Home Away. I was there from July and was supposed to be there only until February, at which point I was supposed to be going home.

"No way. I will not be going home," I said. And on January 20, I left.

Actually, it was over Thanksgiving that I made up my mind that I was never going home. This is what happened: Melissa, my sister, and I were arguing in the kitchen. My dad grabbed Melissa by the back of the hair and threw her up the stairs. Twelve stairs. He literally threw her up all of them. He told her to stay in her room. Melissa and I are only a year and a half apart. It's not that uncommon for us to fight. I didn't think anything of it.

"Well, Jesus Christ," I thought, "if that's what he's going to do to her, if that's what he's going to do to me every time I step minorly off his path of the way we're supposed to live, no way." I was not going home. I kept thinking to myself, "Imagine what would happen if I ever lipped off to him."

I told all the counselors at Home Away. I told my therapist. I told my social worker. One of the therapists called my dad and told him what I said.

My dad said, "Well, fine, if she wants to be on her own let her be truly independent. Let her go through things—Christmas and New Year's and her birthday—alone."

I said, "Okay, let him be that way."

When everybody went home for Christmas with their parents, I stayed at Home Away. When everybody went home for New Year's with their parents, I stayed at Home Away. For my birthday, I was at the group home. At Christmas I called and said, "Merry Christmas." That was all. I hung up. New Year's I called, said, "Happy New Year's," and hung up. I was going to call on my birthday and see if they would tell me happy birthday. Finally, I said, "Screw that idea," and I waited for them to call me. Well, they never called.

My parents are on welfare. They ended up getting something like eight hundred and some bucks a month. They pay fifty dollars to rent a five-bedroom house because they had help from HUD and neither of my parents work. My mom gets food stamps and the welfare check and medical assistance. They know my dad lives there. The only reason they're letting my dad be there is my dad is forty-nine years old. He's old enough to be my grandfather.

The Runaways

My dad's Mexican and he dropped out of school because his mother died when he was nine. He started working when he was eleven. So he never finished his education. He isn't working now. My dad's trade is sheet metal, but now they use only computers. Since he had no knowledge of computers, he got laid off. He's teaching himself computers. My step-mom's brother-in-law gave him one, charged him $1,000 for a $2,400 machine. It took him damn near a year to get it paid off. He's also going to the University of Minnesota right now. Got a grant. He's hoping to get into the technical part of it, 'cause right now, okay, people who go for the classes he's going for are considered low-life scum. They're on welfare and getting grants from the government. But if you go to the technical institute at the University, you're like worshipped, you're way up there. He wants to get up there. He's got his GED, cost him twenty-five dollars through classes at the junior high a block away from where we live. He passed all the tests. He got every question right.

I believe my dad is an alcoholic. When things get too much for him, he starts drinking. But that's about the only time. When he gets really angry or really depressed, he'll drink.

The first time my dad beat me, it was basically because of a miscommunication. He asked me if my sister had taken a shower. I said, "I don't know, ask her." He was sitting out in the living room. My bedroom was maybe one hundred yards from where I thought he was sitting. I was sitting there thinking about it for a few seconds. My back was towards the door. I didn't see that he had gotten up and was outside my bedroom door. I yelled so he could hear me, "I don't know, ask her." He came in super mad and started punching me and saying, "Don't ever yell at me again."

Right now, I just run around with a cut on my left eye and I have a nice bruise.

When I was born my dad had a master plan for my life. When he found out I didn't want to follow his master plan, that I wanted to go to cosmetology school, he got seriously upset. He wanted me to be a scientist. I'm sorry, I have no interest in science. I go to class, pass the class with a C. I'd rather do people's hair and make-up. It's more fun. I like doing that. 'Cause then they go, "Oh, my God, that looks so good. Thank you very much." And then they have to come back to me to do it 'cause they can't ever do it right.

This time, when my parents threw me out, I didn't have no place to go. But if you're outgoing on the street, and you're careful while you're outgoing, you can meet just about anybody. Then it's about the time when you're living on the street. It doesn't matter if you're Vanna White. You're just a person.

On the streets, I walk around, watch people I know if I know anybody. Sometimes I go down to Project Offstreets. Most, after they've closed, I go uptown to Embers. When I start getting tired, that's when I'm like in really big trouble, really screwed, literally, because I don't have any place to sleep. The night before I was up all night.

The Runaways

In January, the day after my birthday, on January eighth, I ran away from Home Away. I was extremely depressed. My parents hadn't called me. I just said screw it and ran away. I got severely drunk with these two guys. That's how we were keeping warm. In an hour I drank half a bottle of root beer schnapps, forty-two proof, half a bottle of whisky, sixty-two proof, and half a bottle of bourbon, one hundred proof. I was in the middle, so they kept passing the bottle to me and, of course, I'd take some. It ended up, we all went to this one guy's house. The first guy, Mark, passed out. Because I was spending the night over there, Mike said I had to do something with him. So I did. I was real lucky I didn't catch anything.

One time, me and my boyfriend stayed over at his best friend's house and his best friend says, "The only way she stays over here is if she does something with me."

I said, "Fine."

With Turner—with him it was basically the same thing. You either put out or you get out. I ask him, "Can I crash?"

He says, "Yeah, but do you want to fuck?"

I say, "Well, I don't know."

"Well, I don't know if I'm going to let you stay here or not," he says.

He tried to rape a friend of mine. He'd screw anything that moves. He'd screw a snake if he could get somebody to hold its head down. I'm serious.

My parents consider it being a whore for the simple reason that you're getting paid for it with a place to stay the night. I guess you could call it being a prostitute. I'm not doing anything illegal. I'm not getting paid for it. They're using you to get their nuts off and you're using them to get a place to stay.

I try to get checked out every three months. If I start to have any symptoms of anything, I go in. If anything starts acting weird, I go in. Just before my parents threw me out the second time, I got checked out. Every time I move back to my parents, they put me back on the welfare grant, back on the medical assistance plan. We pay for it that way.

I do worry about catching AIDS or some disease, because there are like two you can't get rid of—AIDS and VD. As a practical joke, I gave my boyfriend a rubber yesterday. I also worry about getting pregnant. See, a lot of people don't know how their bodies work. Me, I do. I'm one who's lucky. And every time I've tried this it worked beautifully. It works out just great. What I do is this: seven days after I've had my menstrual cycle, I'm safe. Three days before I go on my menstrual cycle, I'm safe. Any time I'm on it, I'm safe. That basically works out perfectly for me. I haven't as of yet had anything go wrong with that system. I waited for four years watching every little change my body went through. I've got it down. I know exactly when everything happens. It's exactly sixteen days after I get off my period before I ovulate.

In sixth grade, we took sex education. In seventh grade, we took biology. Part of that was sex education. I got an A in it. I knew all the answers. If there was a question that I didn't know the answer to, which happened very rarely, I'd ask my mom. Because I got an A, people tought, "Oh, my God, Mira must be a slut, she knows all the answers." I'm like, "No, Mira's still a virgin even." You know, hey, Mira was a virgin up until last year.

I had problems with my self-esteem when I was a kid and most of the time through high school until I dropped out. Then I started making it out on my own, making all my friends. Lately, I've been thinking about all the people that I knew in high school who had money and who were well off, the ones who used give me crap all the time. And I thought to myself, "If they were here with me or had the same problems that I'm having now, they would never have been able to take it as well as I did." That made me feel pretty damn good about myself. I could do what they couldn't, yet they had the balls to give me crap because I wasn't as good as they were. That really helped me with my self-esteem. But when I'm in the situation of put out or stay out, or put out and get out, I do put out.

I dropped out of school the first time my parents kicked me out. I had been in Home Away. I was getting straight A's and B's. I had one C. Four A's. Oh, God, my grades were four A's, A C, and a D. Those were my final grades for trimester one, God. I remember the grades because those were the first four A's I'd gotten in the first trimester in a long time. I did not tell my parents. They still don't know to this day that I got four A's.

As far as they're concerned, I was failing all my classes like last year, my sophomore year. They thought maybe I needed easier classes. They had me take these tests. My tests results came back and said I should be graduated and a freshman in college. I thought, "This is not helping me get easier classes."

I've always had the capability to excel above average students. I always have gotten A's, but I was never trying. I just said, "Screw it." I know I can, and my teachers know I can, and my parents know I can. Why do I have to show off to the rest of the students. I get shit from two thousand students—"you geek, you nerd"—because I get better grades they they do.

So, I had all these good grades going for me at the beginning of my junior year. In the second term I started sloughing off. I figured, "What the hell, I soared above the eagles, why do I have to show off and do it again?" I started getting B's and C's my second trimester because I wasn't trying as hard. Then, in January, as I said, I ran away from the group home because they were going to send me home in February. I was gone six weeks and dropped out of school. If I had gone to school, they would have picked me up on a court order and brought me back to the group home.

When I was home again, I went back to school. But I kept getting these urges to run away. I didn't want to do that. I skipped school two days in a row to go talk to my best friend, my personal shrink. My parents found out that I skipped school those two days and they got highly upset.

Just to prevent us from skipping school, my dad drives us to school, drops us off, watches us walk into the building, then comes to pick us up after school. Well, me being as crafty and sneaky as I can be, I let him drive me to school. As soon as my dad would pull off and the bell rang and everybody was on the way to class, I'd walk out the door and get the eight-fifteen bus to Minneapolis. I'd stay for an hour and come home. If I stayed for more than an hour, I'd be screwed. I'd miss my dad. So, everything worked out. At least, I thought it did.

Both days I managed to get back to school a half hour before school was over. Dad didn't know that first day. He found out the second day. My sister's boyfriend's mother saw me at the bus stop. My parents and I got into that argument the next day. I finally told my dad that what was making me so mad was that he was living my life and wasn't letting me live it.

I said, "Why are you forcing me to accept the things you think and feel instead of letting me? After all, it is my life."

He said, "Basically, what you're saying is, 'Fuck you, Dad.' "

"It's not what I've been saying," I said, "but it's what I'm saying now."

That was it. That blew the whole thing, right there. He kicked my ass, then he dropped me at the corner of University and Central.

He said, "Don't call home. Don't show up there. Don't do anything."

He said, "I don't want to hear from you again."

Now, I stay wherever I can whenever I can. In these last two and a half weeks, I've had a place to stay, an actual apartment to sleep in, five or six times, maybe. But other than that it's like wherever I start passing out is where I pass out.

I don't really have to eat. I do when I can. Otherwise, it doesn't really bother me. I've gone six weeks without eating anything. That was the first time I ran away. The people I was living with didn't have enough money to even feed themselves, but if they bought a loaf of bread, I'd get the tail end. They were struggling. They were trying to get married because Julie was pregnant with this kid. She was sixteen, he was twenty-one. They were basically in the same boat I was.

Any rate, I'd take the two tail ends of bread, you know, and toast them or eat them dry. I never liked sitting down and eating a complete meal after that because, first off, I'd get a stomach ache and, second off, I'd be craving food for like the next four days. That made it all the harder on me.

For that six weeks I wasn't eating, I would go up to the store and rip off two or three packs of cigarettes and bring them home. There were some days when I'd come out with two pounds of chopped meat for dinner. Since I ripped it off, the couple I was staying with would give me a hamburger. But I didn't want to eat a whole meal because I would be dying for four days trying to get some food. The more you worry about it, the more you realize, "Jesus Christ, I'm hungry. What am I going to do?" Then you mow the lawn with your teeth.

It made me feel guilty, stealing. But I figured, you know, there's so much money the government spends on nuclear weapons. Did you ever look at the pricing range on like the MX missles or government aircraft. There are toilet seats that cost two hundred dollars. That's pushing it as far as I'm concerned. If they were to take half the money they spent on war, they'd probably feed . . . but they don't bother. They burn all this excess food, they bury it. With all the food that they waste, and the money they spend on unneeded things, they could be feeding thousands of people, not only in Minnesota, but all over.

My personal goal is to get general assistance. If I can get general assistance for one month and get an apartment, I can get a job. Every time I go out and apply for a job I've gotten one within two days. So all I've got to do, really, is get enough money to rent an apartment for one month and I'm set. But you can't get a job without an address. For two and a half weeks I've been looking for somebody that I can stay with for a month so that I can put an address on an application. But I haven't found anybody. That's why I'm still living on the streets. It's like everybody I know says, "Sorry, we can't," you know. I'm like, "Hey, no problem. Don't worry about it. I've made it so far. No big-ee."

Lately, I've been going up to Project Offstreets. If I haven't slept, I'll eat and sleep all day, to catch up on sleep. Right now, my brain is not wanting to function because I haven't slept. Last night I was sleeping on the cement floor underneath some stairs of an apartment building. The only reason I was sleeping there was because it was a lot warmer than it was outside. If it would've been warmer, I probably would've stayed up all night again. Sleeping on a cement floor is not the most comfortable place to sleep.

I really don't care where I live as long as it's a place of my own—with my name on the lease, my name on the door and my name on the mailbox.

I'd love to end up as a cosmetologist, maybe get my bachelor of arts degree, because that helps. First I'd have to get my GED. The only thing I can't do when it comes to cosmetology is cut hair. Trimming I can do, but cutting it so that it's a new style is the only thing I haven't learned how to do yet.

A lot of times I think, "Why is it so rough? Why is my life so rough when all that I actually really and truly ever think about is finding somebody that I can care about and that will care about me?" You know, a relationship that will last a long time. It's a simple thought, but it's an impossibility. It never happens.

The Runaways

You see my old man's got a problem
He live with the bottle that's the way it is
He says his body's too old for working
I say his body's too young to look like his
My mama went off and left him
She wanted more from life than he could give
I said somebody's got to take care of him
So I quit school and that's what I did

You got a fast car
But is it fast enough so we can fly away
We gotta make a decision
We leave tonight or live and die this way

—"Fast Car"
TRACY CHAPMAN

Linda, 16

"So I figured I would go somewhere and start a new life . . . But New York is not exactly like I pictured it."

The Runaways
81

My mother got involved with a guy who was very bossy. Before he came, things were cool. I didn't even think about running away —had no reason to. I was very happy. Before he came, I could say that I had a family. Now I don't, because he don't like me and I don't like him. No matter what I do he's always there to make me wrong.

He'll just mess with me, you know? Tell my mother different things that I do—to try to get me into trouble or somethin'. Most of the time I ignore it, but dig it—dig it, not long. You can't ignore too much. He's been doing things all along, you see, but it's just the fact that when I get to my breakin' point, when I can't take anymore, instead of physical changes, I felt as though I'd just leave. And that would save both of us pain, or somebody gettin' hurt.

My mother knows. I told her. I told her once and that didn't do any good, so I just said the hell with it. To a certain extent she acted like she was concerned but if she was really concerned she would of at least put forth effort to put a stop to it. As far as I was concerned, there was no change. Things are still going on.

My mom can call up crying and all that, but she wasn't crying when she told me to get the hell out. She wasn't crying then. She ain't seen me in about two or three weeks, so now she's gonna
start cryin'. It's not that she didn't care about it, it's just that she needed somebody to feel close to, you know. Somebody to love her, I guess. I'd like to just see him pack his clothes and say, "Goodbye!" and there wouldn't be no need to run away. Unless . . . unless my mom might start going off. But I feel this way: he could still be her boyfriend, take him someplace else.

Dig it, I been kissin' ass all my life. All my life people have been sayin', "You know, Linda is such and such" and things. And no matter what I believe in, I have to drop what I believe for someone else's pleasure. I'm tired of that, you know? It's about time for me to start thinking about my happiness, and what I want to become. Don't drop my thoughts for somebody else. I'm tired of that. I missed out on a whole lot of cake doin' that.

So I figured I would go somewhere and start a new life. Just a spur of the moment thing. I would run away, come to New York, find a nice job or somethin', you know? And probably about eighteen or nineteen, I'd go visit my mother again just to let her know I'm alive. But New York is not exactly like I pictured it would be. New York is about a lot of hustlin' and stuff and I'm not about to . . . I may sell a few drugs here and there, but the rest of that stuff is just too deep for me. I can't get into that.

Dig it, if you want to run away, you have to have a place to go and money, place to eat, sleep, wash. And you have to be able to take care of yourself if you run away. You have to be able to really take care of yourself. People turn into junkies, people turn into prostitutes, they just literally go off, you know, because they do just about anything to survive. Others—they feel as though it's just too hard and too cold out there, so they commit suicide. You have people who commit suicide because they can't make it. You have other people who sell their bodies and make it. Me, myself, I wouldn't sell my body. That was a gift to me. Why sell a gift?

For those who want to run away, try to hold on, 'cause the world is cold, and people will knock you down just so they can get up top. They'll knock you down and have you sellin' your own body, puttin' money and food in their own pockets.

You know, a lot of times pimps will come over and act like they want to be your friend, but they don't want to really be your friend. A lot of people slipped by that. All you got to do is listen to his rap. Check out how he's dressed and acts and everything. If he comes up and is sayin' to you, "Do you have a man?" or somethin' that you usually don't be sayin' to a friend. Or just check him out if he wants to buy somethin', 'cause a pimp, man, they'll go overboard. They'll go out and start spending thousands, you know. They'll spend some money and before you know it, you'll be payin' them with either your life or as their moneymaker. They'll slick you into it. Pimps are slicker than goose shit, I swear! They are!!!

You'll be walkin' around lookin' like dirt, dig it. Check that out. While he's ridin' around in this big old car throwin' off his diamond rings and whatnot, you're walkin' the streets lookin' like hobo's grandmother! You don't need nothin' like that. You know, a person come out into the street and they don't know nothin' about the street. All they want is a place to go, a place to eat. That line right there, that "baby" trash—they'll fall for that in a minute. That's because they're hungry and cold.

And another thing, man, you become a prostitute and by the time you're thirty-five or forty, your body is so messed up, it's been used so much, that if you do want to find a man, they're not gonna want you. Who's gonna want someone whose body is all messed up and used and everything? Dig it! that was a gift, a gift from God. You know what I mean?

See, when Odetta and I came here, we knew we had to make money somehow. We knew we didn't want' to give our body up. We had money for about a week or so. When we came here we didn't have anything, and now we're about to go home and we don't have anything, but there's not a day that we went without going to sleep. You know, man, I hid us somewhere because we always had someplace to sleep. We slept one night in a hotel. Dig it, we had to sleep one night on a train. We ran into a couple of people, very nice people. In fact, there was a girl that picked us up to go to her house.

The Runaways

If you're going to run away, the best of luck to you. Make sure you got everything—money, clothes, a place to stay. Make sure your game is packed. Just don't get caught. It's embarrassing as hell to have to walk back into the house after you've run away and have to say, "Hey, I couldn't do it."

About my future? I don't know. I mean, I might be here today and gone tomorrow. I might be here now and gone at seven o'clock. You know, I don't know.

The Runaways

*But I reckon I got to light out for the territory
ahead of the rest, because Aunt Sally she's going
to adopt me and sivilize me, and I can't stand it.
I been there before.*

—The Adventures of Huckleberry Finn
MARK TWAIN

Odetta, 15

"My stepfather hits me. I can't hit him back because I'm not as big as he is."

The Runaways

Linda and me have the same problem. I have a stepfather, too. And we're in the same thing, same exact thing. I figure she don't have to take it, why should I have to take it? I don't have to take nothin' nobody gives me.

My stepfather hits me. I can't hit him back because I'm not as big as he is. He just hits me with one hand and I'm gone. He's a Leo, right? And some Leo men I don't get along with. He's one of them that I don't get along with. He has a thing that he wants everything done when he says do it, and how he wants to do it. No other way. Just the way he said to do it, right then and there. And if you don't do it, he always hollers at you, and he makes you nervous and shit. He got my brother. He got my little brother really shook up—does things no other kid would do just because of him always hittin' him and shit. That's why he's like that.

You know my mom bends down and he kicks her. He'll whip the fuck out of my mom, and my mom says, "Yeah, I'm not stayin' with him no more," and then the next minute she's there kissin' his ass, and I can't stand that. She gets her ass almost killed and shit, you know, bruises all over her; she's gonna bend down and kiss his ass.

I would never put my kids down for a man, you know? Never in my life. Check that out. That's what my mom said: "My kids always come before you." Well, it never was like that. He always came before us. Like if I asked my mom for one little dime—it's hard for me to get money out of my mom, you know? I don't get no money to buy clothes or anything. Right now, I don't have no clothes. Somebody stole my clothes. I had clothes, but it would be once in a blue moon I would be able to get this and get that and go there. She would act like I would do something every day. You know, go out every day, like it's a habit. It's not a habit, it's just once in a blue moon.

"Can I go to this party?"

"What time is it? When does it start? Will you come home this time?"

"You act like I been to parties day after day, day in and day out."

It don't work like that.

I'm scared to ask my father anything. I have to get up a lot of courage to ask my father anything because he might come out with, "Hell, no," or a smack, 'cause you said somethin' wrong. That's how he is, and I can't stand him.

He's the type if he's smilin' then everybody else has to be smilin' and if he's frownin' . . . That's a lot of shit because if I want to frown, I'm gonna frown, and if I want to smile, I'm gonna smile, no matter when it is. I don't have no time clock on my lips tellin' me what to do.

The Runaways

I have an older sister, Ann. She ran away when she was fourteen years old and she never came back. She said she wasn't comin' back neither. And she ain't never come back until now. She got kicked out of the place, but she didn't really want to come back home. The same day my mom got on me, she got on Ann for nothin'. My mom really started going off, and I didn't really do nothin' to her, did I?

When I was young, I had to go into the home just because we had to move. We moved into my grandmother's house and a lot of people in my family was living with my grandmother, you know? My mom just decided that somebody had to go into the home, two people had to go into the home. Two people, out of all these people, had to go into the home. If that's the case, nobody should have went into the home, you know? We wasn't poor. It was just this thing that everybody was staying at my grandmother's, right? My uncle, my aunt, and us—like three generations.

Me and my other sister had to go into the home, and that home was really rough. They give you less of everything. They don't like to give up anything. They just like to get the money coming in.

I don't know why my mother put me in a home, 'cause I have two brothers who are mentally retarded and they're in a home. She took good care of us. Really, I don't know why she did that. Once you really sit down and think about it, there was no reason for it, putting us in a home, because who could have took care of us. She's taking care of us now. It was a big house, too, you know? It has a basement, first floor, second floor, and then an attic. There was a lot of room there, a lot of room to sleep—the den, basement. Basement was nice, too. Basement—a lot of people sleep in the basement, upstairs on the floor, anywhere, you know?

I don't think no parents should ever put no one in a home whether they can take care of them or not. It's hard to explain how I felt. I did feel something. I felt like I was left out, like she didn't want me no more—puttin' me in a home. Don't throw your kids off on somebody that you don't even know. That's why they need protection.

As far as me going back home, they can take me back home as many times as they want to. But if I don't want to stay there, I'm not staying. I'd probably go in their house, but that don't mean I'm going to stay in their house and sleep there.

I'll go home and ask my mom how she's doin' and everything, and then I'm going to break down too and tell her I'm not staying. You know, "I came here to see how you are because I don't want to be kissing your butt and I don't want to be kissing his butt." I want it to be that when I go back home, I'll be able to walk in and say, "Mom, I left and I did so-and-so for myself, and I made it. I made it, you know? I live over here now." I'll tell her, "Yeah, Mom, I'm livin' in California now. Would you like to come and see my place? Come see me."

The Runaways

89

KITTY: I dream of home. Christ,
I always dream of home.
I've no home. I've no place.
But I always dream of all of us together again.
We had a farm in Ohio.
There was nothing good about it.
It was always sad. There was always trouble.
But I always dream about it as if I could go back. . . .

—"The Time of Your Life"
WILLIAM SAROYAN

Part Three

The Back-To-Schoolers

All of these kids had returned to so-called alternative, opportunity or continuation schools, where they got their last chance to earn a high school diploma in the public school system. There are hundreds of schools like these throughout the country and each one serves a very different purpose, though their effectiveness has received little serious evaluation.

Kids at these alternative schools couldn't survive or succeed in the normal public school environment. They were failing classes or had discipline problems; they had been in trouble with the law—often for selling drugs—or couldn't live with their families.

Most of the students we talked with were doing remedial work. They were unhappy about that. They showed us their basic multiplication workbooks and said, "Why are they giving us baby stuff?" They felt stigmatized, undervalued and ashamed of where they went to school. They felt that they weren't "making it," and desperately wanted to be like other teenagers attending regular high school.

By and large, these kids were fiercely opinionated, angry, rebellious, loud and foul-mouthed. They attend small, individually-focused classes much like in expensive, private schools. Why shouldn't that encourage them? Because they're not treated as special, they're treated as a problem. It was our impression that most of their classes underestimated their maturity, undervalued their intelligence and undermined their potential.

The Shawnee Missions Alternative High School in Kansas City is a notable exception.

That was where Carrie, a bright and bubbly teenager who had previously gone to several public schools, was enrolled. When her parents were divorcing, she became increasingly depressed and disturbed. She dropped out of school and was hospitalized for several weeks. After her discharge, she entered Shawnee Missions. Like other students we interviewed there, she was enthusiastic about her teachers, principal, and school. They felt the school's staff genuinely cared about them.

Lawrence attended the Dag Hammarskjold Alternative Junior High School in San Francisco. Unlike most alternative schools, it is only for seventh and eighth graders. It strives to be a kind of safety net, catching students with serious problems before they enter high school and become unreachable.

In our roundtable discussions at Dag Hammarskjold, the availability of drugs was the kids' chief concern. Around every corner, they said, pushers were waiting. And almost all the students acknowledged that they were among those who sold drugs—coke, crack, grass, anything.

Charles and Joshua both attended the Dallas Alternative Career Center, where students must have full-time jobs to be accepted and must maintain them until they graduate.

*Teen Editors: Julie Horowitz
                  Elspeth Steiner*

Carrie, 17

"Some schools, the teacher is just like, 'God, another day!'
These teachers, they seem like they want to be here."

The Back-To-Schoolers

I think that the hardest thing about going from elementary school to junior high school probably everywhere is that in elementary school, the teachers are liking it—they enjoy teaching. In junior high school, they start to bum out a little bit on it.

I was an accelerated student in elementary school. When I got to junior high, they put me in advanced classes. That's when my emotional stability kind of went freaky on me. It started building up then.

My parents separated when I was in fourth grade. I didn't have much memory of my dad anyway. He wasn't the type of father who stayed home a lot. So I pretended—in a way, fantasized. It's not so much that I was out of it and couldn't deal with reality. I just totally blocked out all my negative feelings and anything unhappy. That's when I started breaking down on my grades and stuff.

The teachers knew that we were having some family problems. They tried to help me out with that. But I guess you could say I was ignoring reality. I wasn't dealing with my problems. A lot of times, I'd just stay after school and my math teacher, he'd talk to me 'cause he'd seen a lot of kids go through divorces. He'd just stay talking with me and giving me support and telling me that things are going to be okay.

By the seventh grade, I realized that not all teachers care. I started partying with some drugs. It didn't help with dealing with reality. I just placed myself in this fantasy world that everything was going to be okay when, actually, my brains were falling and I started using a lot of drugs, and so did my brother.

And my mom wasn't very happy. I was just ignoring all those things, you know. We had to move out of our house that we'd lived in for ten years, and that really made me angry. That was 'cause of the divorce. The amount of money my dad paid us for support was not enough. We had high bills because the house was in bad shape. We hadn't kept up with it. So I had a lot of anger directed at him for that.

I didn't want to move out of the house. It was unfair that he could live in a nice house and we had to move into an apartment. We moved and kind of got settled in. That was my eighth-grade year.

By the time we really felt settled, I was in the ninth grade and entering Blue Valley High School. That's when he popped a custody suit on us, and I broke down, really. I had held a lot of bad feelings towards him, a lot of anger and stuff. I did okay at the beginning of the school year because I really liked my teachers at school.

But it was hard because all these kids had a lot of money and a lot of nice clothes, and I didn't. I was living right on the borderline in the only type of apartment building that was in that school district. The rest were all huge houses. I felt like an outcast. I was used to being liked in school. I had grown up with a lot of kids at the other school. All of a sudden, I was with kids that I don't know, and they don't seem to care to know me. I started bumming out on that.

It just made me not want to go to school. It made me want to leave class and go to the bathroom and smoke a cigarette. Plus, I don't think I was ready for high school yet. It was really crowded and I was nervous, too. I didn't have any friends there to help give me the courage to be myself, you know? To really get along with people.

Things just kinda built up. I was missing more and more days. It got so bad that when I would wake up in the morning, I would feel sick. I would literally get sick. And then my mother would calm me down and put me back to bed. I'd wake up in the middle of the day and I'd feel fine. But then every morning before school, my body would get sick. I don't know what they call that. There's some psychological term for it.

I was lucky if I went to school three days a week. A couple of times, I went to the nurse's office and just laid down and cried. Kids looked at me like—you don't belong here if you're not going to be coming into school. And rumors started. This is what really made me mad, 'cause I didn't know anybody there. Rumors started going around that I was pregnant, that I was running off to a different country with some freaked-out guy. It was real elaborate.

At first, it was kind of a joke. I just kept hearing more and more of it. And it really made me angry. Here's these people that didn't give a damn to know me, but then once the problem started happening, they were more than willing to talk about me, to put me down.

And there was this custody suit gong on, so if I didn't go to school, my dad would surely get custody for us. The custody suit was in the summer before school of my ninth-grade year. There was a three week period in the summer that the judge made my brother and me go over to my Dad's for a trial basis.

Well, the first night there, my dad started accusing my brother of having a pot pipe and smoking dope at my grandparents. Yeah, we got high. Yeah, we had paraphernalia. But the way we feel about our grandparents, we didn't do that. You know, 'cause your grandparents would totally freak out. They wouldn't understand it and they'd be hurt. So we didn't bring any with us. It really made us mad that my dad would accuse us of being high out there. We just thought if we did that, then we would be low-lifes.

So we left his house that night, the first night, when he was asleep, about two o'clock in the morning. We walked about three and a half, four miles, to the nearest telephone and called my mom to come pick us up.

The next morning, we got woken up to my dad and step-mom banging on our front door. My mom answered the door. My step-mom called my mom a drunk and she called her a bitch. I don't remember what else she said. I just started crying and freaking out on it.

I was too scared to go out of there. I opened the window. I saw their car right below. So I started throwing everything. I threw everything that my dad had ever given me out the window.

He knocked on my door.

"Carrie, come on," he said.

"I ain't going nowhere with you!" I said.

Finally, he left. He went out to the car. He saw all this stuff. And he started picking it up off his car and setting it down.

"You might as well get rid of that shit," I yelled, "because I don't want it. I don't need it."

Then he went and got a court order. The law did say we were supposed to be over there for three weeks.

I spent time at my friend's house, and he went over to my friend's to pick me up. I sat there and I read the whole court order before I would go anywhere with him. Just to make sure it was completely legal.

I was so mad at him. He didn't know I smoked cigarettes or anything. I was so pissed off, I didn't care what he thought. I just got my purse, lit my first cigarette, and let his eyes pop out. He told me to put it out.

And I said, "No."

I said, "I may have to live with you, but I'm not going to listen to you."

We're a lot better now. We're a lot more realistic with our feelings, not holding them back. I'd say our relationship is good now. But then it was the pits. I didn't like him. I didn't respect him. I didn't care to see him or anything.

My mom had talked about putting me into Shawnee Mission Hospital for depression. She explained to me a little bit about what they do. She asked me if I'd like to give that a try. I thought about it for a couple of days and I decided I needed it.

I only saw my doctor once because he made a pass, kind of. I don't know if it was a legitimate pass, but I took it that way. I refused to see him the rest of the time. I've heard that he's made passes at other persons, too, which didn't make me feel good about going to the hospital. So I mainly just talked to his nurse.

The Back-To-Schoolers

It was a mental vacation, I'd say. I was with people who had problems similar to mine and worse than mine. I could sit back and say, "Hey, I'm not so bad after all."

I really didn't get my head together until finally my dad came up to visit me. I wouldn't see him at first. Finally, I said okay. My dad came up. We sat down, and he started talking like he had not done anything wrong at all. Like he had been a really good father.

This day, I barely remember it. I don't remember any times with him except for when he was drunk. I don't have a good memory. But I got mad at him because he was acting like he was a perfect father or something. I just tore out and started yelling at him and letting him know exactly what I feel. I started to remember some times, some really bad times, and I started letting all those out. I just carried on for about two hours. I had the staff around to make sure that I didn't go off on him and start hitting him.

As soon as I got done, my dad looked at me real stern-like and said, "Don't you ever, I mean ever . . ."—I thought he was going to say "talk to me like that again"—and he said, ". . . hold anything back like that again."

And that made me feel real good. Because he knew that a lot of what I said was right and he had been denying it, himself. That helped our relationship out a lot, and I was able to talk to him a lot more.

My mom kept in touch with my school counselor while I was in the hospital. They had a school there. When I got out of the hospital, I wasn't doing very well at all. I was pretty messed up. My mom got it set up for me to go here to this school.

I started here my ninth-grade year, second semester. I love it. I do. Of course, there's parts about every school that kind of bug you and get on your nerves, but you've got to accept those things.

It's a friendly school. A lot of people think that we've got kids here that are going to go out and kill somebody with guns. Yeah, there are kids here that steal. And yeah, in the past there were kids that have been very violent. It's like they've been able to get the kids to be more mellow, not so violent and all. I'd say now there's not really any violent person here. You know, somebody would walk in and might see something like a guy who wears beads, has long hair and looks like a Harley rider. They might be scared of him, but he's the nicest guy there.

What's in the future? Junior college. I'm not really sure. That's a lot of what I've been thinking about lately. I'm interested in getting into the medical field, and that's a lot of school, a lot of information. I'm not exactly sure how ready I'd be for that. I might as well get into something a little bit simpler, or just build up, like take courses and get into the job as, say, a receptionist. Take courses as I'm working there. That's probably what I want to do.

I'm getting ready to take this test in my counseling class to help me direct myself a little bit. I'm going to schedule an appointment with the guy that's the counselor there at the college.

When I look at kids at school, there's hardly any with parents all together. A lot have older brothers or sisters that were dropouts. There are some girls—pregnant teenagers— whose mothers were pregnant teenagers. It's really strange. I think the family life definitely influences it.

I wouldn't support the idea of dropping out. I would support the kids, though, and see what is troubling them, why they want to drop out. I'd do my best to keep them in school, to find at least some type of schooling that they would like to stick with. If they kept on insisting on dropping out, then I would make them sit through school until they knew exactly what they were going to do when they dropped out.

I don't mean just work at a gas station, either. You don't drop out to go to work at a gas station. I know some kids that've dropped out and they're doing really well. They just couldn't deal with the high school. But they're still going to have problems getting jobs because people are going to look at them like, hey, you couldn't stick with high school, how are you going to stick with this job?

When it comes right down to it, teachers make the biggest difference in dropping out. A lot of times kids will want to drop out and they'll say something to the teacher, and the teacher tries to tell them not to. A lot of the time, they'll just blow it off. I think if the teacher and kid have a good relationship from the beginning, then that teacher's opinion would be very valuable to the kid. But if the teacher hadn't been there throughout the school year for the kid when the kid needed him, then he's not going to value the opinion at all.

The best part of this school is the staff. They all seem to want to be here. Some schools, the teacher is just like, "God, another day!" These teachers, they seem like they want to be here, pretty much in upbeat, crazy moods. They seem a lot younger. They are younger than most teachers, attitude-wise, too. They keep free spirit. And they're open-minded. I sit with a few teachers and some kids at lunch and jerk around. They can be excellent teachers because they know how to teach so you understand. At the same time, they can be silly so you can enjoy their company. They're real honest with you, too. If they're having a bad day, and you're being a jerk to them, they'll tell you, "Hey, I don't need this."

The people who really know this school—the way it works and how a lot of students are doing better—respect it. But for the people who don't know much about it, except in terms of the teenage mothers and drug-users here, it's got a bad reputation. A lot of kids out there need to go to a school like this. Their parents think they don't belong here because they're not a druggie and they're not a teenage mother. And that's not what it is.

I think that in all schools I'd like to see some better teacher/student communication. The enthusiasm to learn is not really there when you get into the high school.

It's the fault of both teachers and students. Because you might have an excellent teacher who's willing to give it her best and some student comes in all wasted, doesn't want to do anything, tells her to fuck off or something. She bums out and loses her desire to teach.

On the other hand, the student can go in there with a great desire to learn, but the teacher is not the best or something. And they bum out the kid, and the kid doesn't learn anything.

We need something like Dropouts Anonymous, where teachers, students, parents, administrators, family members all get to talk about it. Because when you think about it, kids don't really drop out because of the school. They drop out because there's some other personal problem that is affecting the way they came to school.

You know, if you can get at the source of the problem, then the kid can still deal with school. But a lot of times, you blow it off and say, "The problem is the school. I'm not right for this place."

Any parent who reads this, please keep an open mind to this school and others like it. Because nobody is perfect and we all do have problems and we all need support. That's what this school's about—supporting.

The Back-To-Schoolers

. . . The day moves me
because you were given back to me.
You died night after night in the years of my childhood,
sinking down into speechless torpor,
and then you were told to leave for good
and you left, for better, for worse, for a long
time I did not see you or touch you—
and then, as if to disprove the ascendance of darkness
little by little you came back to me
until now I have you, a living father
standing in the California sun
unwrapping the crackling caul off a cigar
and placing it in the center of his mouth
where the parent is placed, at the center of the child's life.

—"June 24"
SHARON OLDS

Morgan, 16

"Money, not pressure, was what motivated me. If you sell drugs, you got money—gold, teeth gold, leather coats, all of this, different pairs of sneakers every day. They look up to that."

The Back-To-Schoolers

When I was sixteen years old, in the eleventh grade, I was administratively dropped out. That means I was kicked out.

They said I was problem student.

My grades were A's and B's. I was in a college preparatory course and all that. They didn't even look at that when they kicked me out. They looked at all the things I did bad and not all the things I did good.

My parents put me in a private school, but the next semester starts in January, so I have to wait until then.

In my tenth grade year I was just doing crazy things, stuff I shouldn't have been doing. Arguing and like that. I wasn't even terrible, not like killing people. I was arguing with teachers and stuff 'cause I had just come to that school. I was into drugs at the time, not doing drugs, selling drugs. Marijuana.

I had a few encounters with the school establishment. Most teachers I got along with, but not all of them. Of course nobody gets along with all their teachers, but teachers wasn't really a problem. It was more up the ladder on the staff, like the principals and stuff like that. I wasn't really able to get along with them on the top and that's the main thing. You have to get along with them. They resented me after that so I guess I did myself in.

The time I got caught I had it on me. So I was sent to an alternative high school, that's the SOS Program for students on suspension, for all the students from around the whole school system.

When you're suspended you have to go there. They talk to you every day, lecture different things, have police come there and check everybody once a week. So I was, hey, they ain't never gonna catch me because I'm not going to bring any in the first place.

I enjoy school and work and all that, so I didn't cut much. The total is about ten, twelve days sickness. Sometimes I just stayed at home, but I didn't really cut class. I enjoy it. Some people don't like school, period. But in my case I do. I like to keep my mind moving. I like the challenges, you know, and so forth.

So I wanted to be there. I was going to my classes every day. But then again, I was still on the drug scene. I didn't use drugs, I just sold them in school and that was really stupid, tryin' to be in the in-crowd—girls, the fast lane. I was excited all the time. I really did it to myself. I used to bring large amounts of money to school, flashin' it in front of girls, all that type of stuff. It wasn't even really me. I was just trying to impress people. And now, if I had to change it, I wouldna' done none of it. I woulda' left it alone.

The Back-To-Schoolers

It's going to be different when I go to private school. I wouldn't mess over there because my mother, she went through all the trouble of sticking with me. She coulda' just got rid of me, say go with your father, whatever. I won't want to do that anyway. I be wasting my money. Believe me, when I get there I stay there for good.

This dropout thing really made me wiser, 'cause if I would be still in school today I might still have been doing some of the things I was doin'. But now I realize that the drug thing, it's okay for a while but it doesn't last. Every drug dealer must get caught.

I was my own destroyer.

I did it to myself and nobody else did it. It was nobody else's fault. It has to do with personality. If you want to be in school, you going to be in school. If not, you find an excuse not to be there, or you going to cause problems so that you won't be there.

In my case, when I was administratively kicked out they told me that I truly didn't want to be in school. They said, "I'm looking at your actions, what you was doing. You don't really want to be in school."

I was like, wow!

Money, not pressure, was what motivated me. I was greedy. Older people can't understand it, but the younger generation that's out now...they respect that. I can't explain it why. If you sell drugs you got money—gold, teeth gold, leather coats, all of this, different pairs of sneakers every day. They look up to that. Like, "Man, I'm hot!" I guess I was looking at that. Now I look at it as stupid because what you have now, when you young and a teenager, it doesn't mean anything. Because you are adult longer than you are a teenager. So that's when it's really gonna count, when you older. It's frivolous now because it doesn't really matter.

I have friends that haven't been in school since fourth grade, third grade. They never will learn, never wanted to go to school anyway. Some people just don't want to. They satisfied with the way they are. It's them, I guess. The family situation and all that, 'cause it's more likely they been taking care of themselves since like the fourth grade, and they had no other choice but to drop out of school.

Say you wake up in the morning and their little sister is standing crying in the house, and their mother is asleep, don't care. You go to school and you are frustrated. You get there and you just start trouble. Kids take problems to school with them.

Newark is right next to New York and New York is the drug capital of the world. It's just so easy to get. Little kids sell drugs, twelve years old, eleven, ten, have money. Some mothers is right along with it. They do it, too. Father do it. Everybody.

In my case my family didn't know. That's why I used the money furiously. I just spent it. I couldn't buy clothes and go home with it. My mother would say what the hell? My family don't like it 'cause in my family nobody's ever done this, never was into drugs. I'm the first black sheep of the family. They say, "What you doin' to yourself?"

I don't really have a communication with my parents. I don't really talk to them as much as I should. I'm somewhat a loner. I keep to myself, keep my thoughts to myself. I don't express myself too much. I didn't have too much communication with my friends. I was thirteen, fourteen when I started, so I wasn't really too stable on the outside world and all that. I just went out in the world and you really can't do that. Your family has to be your best friend.

If the communication would have been there, I don't think I would have gone out to drugs. I can't say I wouldn't have, but I don't think so. But money, it's like a drug. It's not like a regular job because you can just go out one day and leave with $300 or $400 in your pocket in a hour. That's like nice, man. So I'm thinking like, man, I don't have to work. I don't have to do nothin'. I just come out here a couple of hours a week and I'm going to be spendin' it easy as it comes.

When I was younger, up to the age of like twelve or thirteen, I was more like you'd say a bookworm, until I start hanging out outside, in the street. I started exploring. I start finding like a high. It's fun, I want to do this again, this new thing that I never experienced before. Some adults looked at me like, "He's terrible, look at him now. I can remember when he was a little angel and now look at him."

I don't look at myself as a dropout. It wasn't my choice. It was bestowed upon me. I didn't have no say-so about it. I deserve the kind of thing I had in tenth grade, when I was sent to an alternative school.

But the recent thing that I was kicked out for, I didn't do anything. It was still that grudge against me from the staff. The year before that, before I went to the SOS Program, they used to confront me. I used to talk negatively, plus I know they really wanted me out of the school because I was a problem. I was supplyin' a lot of stuff. I knew I was a problem myself. So when I came back to school they had a grudge against me. They was messin' with me. I was in the vicinity of somebody else that had somethin' and they said, "You definitely had something to do with this, so you out." And the person that has the stuff on them, they get back in school and I'm not. And I was just in the vicinity. They like a D, F student and I was on all honor classes in school.

I don't know what profession I want to take up, what career. I know definitely that I'm going to be in a ROTC program when I get out of high school. If I do go to the ROTC program that means they pay for my college education, tuition and all that, and I just owe them a year's service. So if I don't like the years' service, after I do my year I can just go about my life. But if I do decide I like it, I can make a career of it.

I don't plan on bein' around in the future, but if I do I have some type of advice to give my little sister, even though it might not be good. I tell her, "Definitely, drugs ain't not it."

It most likely won't do her any good 'cause if you think in your mind you want to do somethin', if you want to explore, you gonna do it anyway, no matter how much your family tell you you not supposed to do this, you not supposed to do that. Even if they tells you not to, you goin' to do it regardless. Like in my case, there's no one in my family involved in drugs. Everybody gets religious. I'm the black sheep of the family, I guess.

The Back-To-Schoolers

Speed of life, fast, it's like walkin' barefoot over broken glass.
It's like jumpin' rope on a razor blade,
All lightning quick decisions are made.
Lifestyle plush, females rush,
This high profile personality, who earns his pay illegally.
Professional liar, schoolboys admire,
Young girls desire, very few live to retire.
Cash flow extreme, dress code supreme, vocabulary obscene.
Definition—Street Player, you know what I mean?

—"High Rollers"
Ice-T and Afrika Islam

Lawrence, 15

"I'm not going to sell drugs for the rest of my life. My dream is to be a highway patrolman."

The Back-To-Schoolers

I go to Dag Hammarskjold. I'm fifteen years old. And that's it. I'm a very normal person.

I don't do no drugs. Some of my friends were selling a little drugs where I was selling drugs at, and every time they would get paid they would say, "I want to get burned."

See, they worked for this dude, and the way he would be paying them is you sell a hundred and I'll give you a dozen. That's twenty dollars. You could get twenty dollars or you could get the rocks. But they didn't want the money, they just wanted the rock. They'd be saying "I'm gonna get burned." It was funny to me. Everytime it would come round to payday they'd just run around, "I'm gonna get burnt. I'm gonna get burnt."

I'm saying, "I'm gonna get me some shoes. New clothes, a jacket, take my girlfriends somewhere or get a rental car." But they're talking about "I'm gonna get burnt." They're already burnt.

It's real important to have money, but you've got to have brains, too. I'll tell you this: to sell drugs you've got to have brains.

Is there anything wrong with using drugs? I'd be telling people not to use them. Like one day it was a kid—he was about my age —and he came around. Now you don't even want to sell no ten piece or nothing, but he only had ten dollars .

I said, "Just go back home and try to get ten dollars."

He said, "I can't, just hopped out the window. I'm gonna get in trouble anyway."

I said, "Well, just go on back home and save your ten dollars for something else."

I'm still growing up, I understand. Some parents don't even care about their kids—they don't want to do for their kids so they ain't doing work or nothing in school. My parents tell me that as long as I go to school they're going to put clothes on my back and money in my pocket, enough for me to walk down the street. And if I want to eat something I can go buy it. I mean, he don't give me like five dollars.

Here's how it came up that I told them I was selling drugs. When you start selling drugs it's called grinding. When you start grinding drugs, naturally you're going to start buying heavy clothes and stuff. One night I went and picked up my clothes from my house and they asked me where did I get all those clothes from. I'm not the kind of person who likes to lie to people. I told them that I was selling drugs.

They told me, "Lawrence, you know it's wrong."

I said, "Yeah, but you kicked me out. You know I had to do something."

He said, "But still it's wrong."

I know it's wrong, but still he ain't putting enough money in my pocket. There are things I want to do.

To succeed in selling drugs you've got to know the right people and you've got to do the right thing. And if you do go to jail, you've got to know the people who are gonna get you out. Even if I do get caught I know this man who'll do you a favor. If you get a record now, when you turn eighteen they'll take it off. They'll wipe it off. When you go to get a job or something they won't know about it. Something happened to me on the weekend and it's going to be on my record 'til I get eighteen, but it's gonna get off after that. I ain't never got caught.

Did I still sell drugs? No, but I'm gonna start back on Wednesday, 'cause I'll be broke then. I'm sick of being broke. I want me a car. You can't take no girl to the movies, you can't take her to the drive-in on the bus.

I want to get a car now. I'm not talking about when I'm old, when I'm an old man. I'm talking about now, when I'm fifteen.

You've got different times when you go through phases in your life. Everybody goes through phases. I'm going through a drug-selling phase right now. Then when I grow up and graduate from school I'll stop selling drugs. I'm just doing it now because when I turn eighteen I'm leaving. Forget parents and forget anything else. I still love them. I'll still walk by the house and say, "How are you doing?" Then I'm leaving. I've got to go be my own.

Really, anything I want, they'll give it to me. They'll put money in my pocket. I want to walk down the street with at least about five hundred or six hundred dollars in my pocket.

Just 'cause kids sell drugs doesn't mean that they're going to do it for the rest of their lives. Some people, in their minds, once or twice in their lives, they have a dream—they know what they want to be when they grow up. In my case, I'm not going to sell drugs for the rest of my life. My dream is to be a highway patrolman. I'm just doing it now 'cause I want the money, 'cause I want a car and my parents ain't going to buy me no car.

The Back-To-Schoolers

Well, honey it ain't your money 'cause baby,
I got plenty of that. I love you for your pink Cadillac,
crushed velvet seats, riding in the back, oozing
down the street, waving to the girls, feeling
out of sight, spending all my money on a Saturday night.

—"Pink Cadillac"
BRUCE SPRINGSTEEN

Charles, 19

"If you don't want to get no education, the best thing for you to do is to start lifting weights and try to be a boxer and fight your way through that world."

The Back-To-Schoolers

You're going to need an education. If you don't want to get no education, the best thing for you to do is to start lifting some weights and try to be a boxer and fight your way through that world.

I quit school 'cause they said I missed too many days. I didn't miss that many days, and I didn't want to repeat another semester. So I told them I was going to quit and they said all right. So I quit.

I skipped two days because you can't miss three. I skipped study hall all the time just to go get high. I was tardy a lot. If you get three tardies, you're absent, too. I think that's what happened. They start saying if you don't come to school, then you're not going to get credit for the whole semester. You'll just have to stay where you're at and you ain't going to be passed. You're not going to flunk. You just gonna stay there, whatever grade you're in—tenth, eleventh, twelfth grade. What happens as the grades get higher, school gets boring and you want to try something else. So you don't go to school. You go to the lake instead and get high.

About two or three of us would come, because if you came out with a crowd, you'd get stopped by the officers on the way down the street. They ask where you're going and you can't say y'all going home for lunch because it ain't lunch time yet. It's more easier to get spotted with a crowd than you and somebody else and somebody else. We go up there and get high and nobody has ever catched us up there. On pot, coke and crystal.

School was boring, because you had so many classes to go to. The fun part was skipping or always doing something wrong. You always have to have some kind of adventure in your life, because if you don't have no adventure, you live a boring life. Just try to get to the park without getting caught by the police is an adventure.

There was this teacher, Mrs. King. Right after we would come back from gettin' high, we would go into her class and it look like she got high too. She was a really young teacher. And she said, "God, you smell kind of like pot today, so you better go sit by the window."

She wouldn't ever send nobody to the office or anything. She was a real cool teacher. You could cuss in there. As long as you do your work. That's just it. That's what she was mainly worried about. When we would finish our work, she would have a TV and a VCR. She would let some of the students bring movies. And we could watch them for the rest of the remaining time. She had your work lined up for the day and everything. It was okay.

If I hadn't dropped out, right now I would be still in junior college working my way up to go to college. I think by the time I reached about twenty to twenty-one, I could

The Back-To-Schoolers

already be in college and looking for a good job instead of being right now going to turn twenty and still in high school.

The good thing about it is everybody has to stop and find out their lives and turn themself around. They're going to find out in the long run that education is a way of life. Everything is now becoming to be computers. Have you seen all the cars now? Everywhere you go you see computers. I say education is just the way to go. You got to stick with it and deal with life. Life is coming hard now. It's good to have a diploma and get a college degree.

That's what I'm trying to say. You gotta stick with your education. You gotta go with it all the way, so when you come looking for a job, you have so many years behind what you want to do, they're more likely to hire you than somebody with a year, two years' experience in that. And you already have four years of college and everything.

You have to go the highest you can, whatever you want to do—electronics, drafting, computer technician. It doesn't make any difference. You gotta just be your best and try. My parents did graduate and everything, but some of my uncles, they didn't graduate. And they're saying try to learn from their mistakes, you know. Keep going to school.

The more experience you have in something, the more education, the more likely you'll be hired for a job. They are hiring all kinds of Chinese people, Mexican-Americans, the ones that come over the border and everything. And that's kind of not right 'cause we live here. We're the ones that built this nation and stuff. We should have the jobs, not somebody else. They have their own country. They need to do something with that. If they need to borrow money, well, then, ask them to help their own selves out. We can't help everybody out. The way they get low pay and everything is 'cause they don't have an education. They come across and they don't know where to go. They'll take any job right away.

Nowadays the jobs are gettin' harder. You have to have some kind of background to go and look for a good job.

Right now I've got a job. I'm hoping to hurry up and get my GED or diploma or whatever you get through this school. And afterwards, just start going to junior college and help me out to go to college. I want to be something like my father. He's graduated from four years of college. And now he's making infrared lenses and stuff. I would like to do something like that. It would hopefully brighten up my life. So when I do get married or if I ever want to get married, I'd have something there for me.

My father, he told me to go to this school, that that would be smart because you're going to regret it more in life when you see all your friends going to college and that's what you want to do. You can't go to college if you don't have no diploma or GED. I decided to come back to school and make myself better and go to college.

If I had a son or daughter, and if they wanted to drop out of school, I think I would go ahead and tell them not to try to get a job and say, "Well, I'm going to make it work. I can make it work. I got an apartment and everything already." 'Cause it don't work out that way.

I'm thinking about me and my parents. I told them that I wanted to drop out of school. At first they got mad. They said, "Well, why do you want to dropout?"

I said, "Because they say I missed too many days and I didn't. I was kinda absent—not absent, tardy a little bit." They never forced me to go to school. The more you force, that's the less they want to do. They never threatened to hit me to go to school or nothing. I went ahead and dropped out and I thought that I could do it all—like getting a job and everything. I found out later that you're going to need to go back to school.

You just try to show them things that they're going to want in life like new clothes, a car, jewelry, a watch, a ring or something like that, you know. Just show them that and they're going to find out they need an education. And plus get a job too. You know, if you're not handicapped. No matter what you do, you're going to need it.

Keep on going no matter how hard it gets. Because in the long run, you'll be like us, sitting at a table talking to y'all. You people are not alone. You gotta learn from other people's mistakes. And that's one thing I didn't do. Learn from other people's mistakes.

The Back-To-Schoolers

124

If I was to pick out middle C on the piano and keep hittin it, thass how it sound when my jography teacher be teachin. I don't listen, just turn her off and stare out the window at sky and freedom, thinkin. I don't listen, just turn her off and stare out the window at sky and feedom, thinkin how it would be if I had finish servin my time and was gone from here with my diploma...or gone without it. Then I'm hearin middle C get louder on my ear, she astin me to repear what she been sayin. I wanna say, "Bitch, I'm tryin not to hear you." But since I got a mother, I'm thinkin jography teacher might be somebody's mother too, so I say, "I didden hear the last part."

Look like she could be decent and repeat it, but she wanta outfox you, so she say, "Tell us what part you did hear." When you don't answer, she flippin through her report book to make another mark gainst your record. I hate school, and that's how come I got to cuttin class and hangin out with those who hate the same.

—A Hero Ain't Nothing But A Sandwich
ALICE CHILDRESS

Joshua, 19

"The only people who I thought cared was the coaches,
but I found out different."

The Back-To-Schoolers

At this time I live on my own. I can make it, but I don't want to just be makin' it. I want to be MAKIN' IT.

My parents never talked to me very much. They went along with anything I said. My mom told me, "You and your brother, you're just wastin' my time. I would really like it if y'all leave."

I was too young to realize that she was really wanting us to go. So my brother and me moved—that was the only way I could make it.

I see her every once in a while. Yet still she's the same way. Now that I'm older, I've tried to talk to her and try to find out why she treated us like that and I draw blanks every time.

When I was fifteen, my father, he was around. But he was more interested in his girlfriends and stuff like that. We could talk to him and he'd come over and see us, but, you know, he has his own life.

I think if my parents cared, I wouldn't be on my own right now. At the age of fifteen, I wouldn't have been stealing cars, either. My mom knew this. This was the only way I could make it at the time, at that age. If you steal a car, you can sell it to a guy. He'd give me like ten thousand dollars for the car.

The guy just walked up to me on the street and told me, "Don't you like this car I'm driving?"

So I told him, "Yeah."

And he said, "Well, I could get you the same car if you do me a favor."

I did the favor for him. I had a little ragged Pinto. He used to have me run drugs to different places for him. When I brought him the money, he gave me my part of it. He got me the car.

At the time, I always thought that I'd get caught doing it. But it was set up to a point to where it was foolproof. I don't know how, but it was just foolproof. My mom wouldn't know. I felt like if my parents cared then, they would have found some way to stop me from doing that or help me out.

I skipped a class every day from my freshmen year. Mostly I stayed out because I wasn't receiving any credits in this class, so I said, "Why go?" I played basketball in school for a while. The only people who I thought cared was the coaches . . . but I found out different. I could be flunking two or three classes, they'll go talk to the teacher an' she'll pass me an' I'll get to play in the games. This was an every six-week thing. And I felt it really hurt me. Doing this so I could play football and basketball. I found out they really didn't care. Mostly all he was worried about was what kind of basketball team they were going to have. He didn't care about the student. He just wanted to be recommended as being the best coach in the ISP or whatever. That hurt me a lot.

I dropped out because I didn't even have my family. I made it though junior high mostly by myself. After my brother died I was on my own. There was a lot of pressure on me. Having to deal with my brother's death was pretty hard. I decided I just wanted to quit, try to get my life straight. When I found out about this school, I said, "Maybe it would work if I could go to work and go to school."

Once I accomplish getting my high school diploma from this school, I have an opportunity to go to college, because when I played football in high school, I had a lot of coaches come. I had one who was concerned about if I wanted to play or not, from Oklahoma State. He calls me when I'm home sometimes and asks me how it's going. He says after I graduate he's going to get me a scholarship. I could play football and go to school. He'll help me out and all with tuition and this kind of stuff. He was a good friend of my father's before my father died. So that's one reason I think he cares about me.

If I want to benefit, if I want to make my life worth living, I'm going to have to go to school to do that, see? First of all, I have to pass the test. Second of all, I have to keep my grades up.

My daughter is nine months old now. I would tell her the kids are seeing new cars and stuff on television and saying they want this and they want that. An' the older she gets, in order for her to have things like this, she has to have an education. If she couldn't understand that then I would find a way to keep her in school. I wouldn't give up.

The Back-To-Schoolers

129

To this extent I'm a stalk.
—How free; how all alone.
Out of these nothings
—All beginnings come.

—"The Longing"
THEODORE ROETHKE

Part Four

———————

The Hangers-In

Almost every kid in every roundtable knew that they needed a high school diploma and an education to make money, to be productive, to succeed. Every one of these kids—including those from the most disadvantaged backgrounds whose parents rarely finished high school—said he or she wanted to complete high school.

Too many, however, seemed totally undernurtured by their families and overwhelmed by premature adult responsibilities. Many never had a childhood. They yearned for parents who would look after them or from whom they could get some encouragement. They longed for teachers who would recognize the effort they made if not their potential. They yearned to express themselves to parents, teachers or friends. Instead, too often there was a void—an absence of parents, an absence of friends, an absence of anyone with whom to share their problems or from whom they could receive support.

Ronica, Noel and Kisha all participated in roundtables at Oakland's Castlemount High School. One educator warned us before our visit that Castlemount was "a bad apple school." We found it to be large and impersonal, and attended predominantly by black students. Public schools often end up being all black, all Hispanic or all white.

Deborah went to Central High School in Kansas City. At the time of CHILDREN'S EXPRESS's visit, Kansas City was under a court order to desegregate its schools. The students—all of them black—who took part in our discussion there vigorously disagreed on whether their school was worse than schools located in white, middle class neighborhoods.

Katina, like many of her classmates at Avon High School in Newark who participated in the roundtable, had already experienced a lifetime of misery, enough to warrant the kind of hopelessness that often leads kids to drop out of school. She came from an alcoholic family and a chaotic home that were hateful to her. She literally couldn't bear to be awake at home and returned there only when she was so exhausted she would immediately fall asleep. Nonetheless, she and her schoolmates were filled with enthusiasm and optimism, and determined to get an education.

Teen Editors: David Katz
Linda Holmes

Ronica, 16

"Just because I fight all the time,
it doesn't mean I act like a boy.
'S 'cause I don't like people."

The Hangers-In

I'm the type of person that everybody would love to be my friend and everything because I used to act all crazy and stuff. I'm cruel and everything. But now I try to straighten up this year.

I've never had an A in my life. I barely got B's. I be trying. It's just some of these teachers that don't want me to learn.

And my mother, she don't understand how much I do try. So I just sometimes give up. You know, she always believes everybody else except me. She says she know me better than I know me. She don't know me. She's trying to make me transfer schools now to this—excuse me, I don't want to sound racist, but—white school. Well, I'm not going to stay there long anyway, because I'm probably going to have to kill everybody at that school if they look at me funny. But my grades are important. They just hard to get.

I have a friend that get real good grades, but she act just like me. I mean, she terrible and everything, but she get straight A's. I don't know how she do it. I wonder how she can be two people at one time. I mean, she bad half the time and then she really get down on that school and all kinds of activites and president of the school. She's real good, but she's bad.

I act all bad and stuff and fighting and all that stuff, 'cause that's the way I grew up. My mother said that's just the way I want to act, but that the way I grew bad. Always gettin' in trouble and stuff. Mostly tryin' to beat everybody up. I don't like nobody saying anything smart. What I think is smart is if they even say anything back to me like, "Well, I wasn't doing this" and all that, they would get slapped. I don't know why. I have a short temper, I guess.

When I do good, nobody remembers. When I do bad, nobody forgets.

The way I act, the way I treat people and the way I talk, that's just the way I am. But I'm good when I really want to be, sometimes.

I ask my mother why do she always remember the bad stuff instead of the good stuff. And then she asks me what have I done good. I can't really tell her. I can't remember.

I like most of my teachers because we're close. I get to talk to them what I can't tell my mother. If my mother find out, she'll get all jealous and mad and stuff.

Most of my teachers, they give me encouragement and help me on passing. I'll come after school. My mother, she really doesn't understand that I be tryin'. My grades don't show it at all. I do be tryin' though.

I don't like my mother to tell my business and all that stuff. "She did this," and all that. I feel that my mother worries way too much, so much she had bad dreams and all that. She thinks the worse of me, calling me all these different names. And my mother don't compliment me at all. It doesn't really make me feel bad. It just that if she scold me, or whatever she does to me, it's not gonna help none. Like kids when they get hit. It's not gonna help them none. It'll make 'em even worse. To me, it seem like that's what happened to my little brother.

My mother never forgets the bad things, like if I be fightin' and I get cut or somethin' like that. She always bring that up in every little conversation. She'll probably say that for the rest of my life, until she die. I wish she just didn't care, not as much as she do. She just care too much for me. She won't give me a break.

I hear some of my friends say, "Me and my mother is best friends." I always say I want her and me to be close. Me and my mother are enemies. I be tryin'. I try to please my teachers, or get on their good side. And they really give me a hard time. It hurt my feelings a lot.

My mother, she do the same thing. I try to get on her good side, and she just start yellin' at me. My mother do get all mad.

"Why you don't come to me?" And all that.

I was goin' off on everybody, just wantin' to beat everybody up. And I did something crazy. I busted my head open. The next day, I went to talk to my counselor, and she was supposed to set up a meetin' with a psychologist. I used to have one when I was a juvenile, and they asked me why I was so bad and stuff.

Then my counselor called my mother and she got all mad and said, "I don't think your problem's all that bad. Why you tellin' them your business instead of tellin' me?"

My mother said to my boyfriend's mother, "I only got sons." She said she gonna rip my pants off and make me wear dresses. I don't act like no boy. Just because I fight all the time, it doesn't mean I act like no boy. 'S 'cause I don't like people.

See, I am the type of person that if I talk crazy, I expect you not to say nothin', just listen to what I got to say. This is the way I am. I don't want nobody sayin' nothin', just get scared. I don't know why I want everybody to be scared of me for some reason. It be wacky. I don't understand myself.

My boyfriend's a dropout. His mother always want me to go to school and she ain't seen his report card since the fifth grade. So I guess she want me to be somebody and stop messin' with him for now. He's supposed to start school, but he's just a dummy. He just got out of jail for dope. But now, he needs either to go to school or do what he was doing, selling dope, because I like somebody to have things if they're going to be with me. I don't like no broke fools.

The Hangers-In

I don't like regular jobs either, so he's going to have to be rich or somethin'. I want him to go back to school, so he'll at least get his high school diploma so when he can't turn to anybody else he can at least get a job. 'Cause he's supposed to be out on his own by now.

My dad used to make real good money. He started to go to college. He's real smart and all that. He just don't want to do nothin' with his life. He sit around the house.

I'm like my father. That's what everybody always say.

They say, "You act like your father more than you act like your mother. Your mother is respectable. She's a working woman."

I still respect him even though he's nothin' no more. If you ain't got no job, you ain't nothing. If you ain't got no money, you got nothin'.

In sixth grade it was fun to learn and all that. Everybody had a group discussion. I wish the teachers now would still have more group discussion with the class and read out loud. They don't do none of that. They just slap you with homework and think you supposed to understand. All they care about is their paycheck, and how about they don't get enough money.

I know a lot of my mother's friends who successfully made it through high school and everything and ain't nothin' now. And people that don't do all that good is somebody. You know what I'm sayin? It's like that. I mean, I may not be gettin' the highest grades, but I know I'm goin' to be somebody some day.

Last year I knew a few people and they was real smart and stuff. The got A's and everything. But now, they don't go to school this year. Their money was doubled this year, so they probably said forget it. My father says there's really nothing wrong with sellin' drugs as long as you don't get too greedy about it. Just make about $10,000 and stop.

Am I going to be in college? I'm not really sure. Probably so. I'm not sure if I'm going to still stick with being a public defender or something like that. That's what I want to be. I want to be inside the court room. Either a clerk or one of the public defenders. Yeah, I'm going to have to.

Anything you want to be, you have to go to school. You want to be out there and have things, gold or whatever it is, you know. You tired of looking like you do and all that other stuff. Money. It seems like you can't do anything without money. Stuff is gettin' way too expensive right now. And everybody want to have the things they want to have, you know?

The Hangers-In

140

I don't know why
I don't know why
Bad luck and trouble follow me
I've tried to be a good boy
It fill my life with misery

—"Bad Luck and Trouble"
Boggie Jake

Deborah, 14

*"When you come to school like this,
they don't have no set order . . .
You just kinda lose your will to learn."*

The Hangers-In

When you get around high school students—that's mostly a majority of blacks—it seems like they not puttin' no progress into the things like they have in the white schools.

They don't seem like they care much about us. We go to our bathrooms. They don't look as nice, which is the students' fault. But you know they could fix them up or try to do something.

After I started coming to junior high school, I didn't like it. I started thinking about it. I said, "Well, you know, I'm not gon' let nothin' stop me. I'll just go ahead. Go ahead and get my education."

The public schools are better where the white kids go. The white people get together, they fight for their kids to have good educations. They say, "We don't want those people in our school." I can see why, because every time we come around, we'll be forever messing up their stuff.

But it seems like somebody could take some time with us and try to give us something like some of the other schools have. We down here, but I would like to go up into one of those schools without paying big money to get some of the education that some kids got. Some things that we don't know, the white kids already know and three times as much.

This is the way I think about it. We can keep up in our books, but the whites are ahead of us because they have them stronger. They have more people in there to assist, and it just seems like it's not fair. Children who come into the classes and play and disrupt the kids who want to learn. They have a conference. If they don't act right, they put 'em out for good. They don't come back. They go find another school.

It was on the news that they first had to get the white people in, the people who were goin' back into the schools. And then the blacks. So in this case, it's the whites get their choice first and the blacks is always back here just constantly trying to fight and get up there.

Because see, it's like this: I did pass. If that's the case, how come I'm still over here when I worked so hard to go there? I have really worked hard last year, the year before and whenever to get to where I wanted to go.

But still there was the first choice of the different races. I figure like this: once you get into a school, your parents can motivate you and you can learn to a point which you want to learn in the schools. But the white people go to their schools. They have nice cafeterias. They have nice bathrooms. They don't have people fightin' all the time. They don't have people cussin' and talkin' ignorant. They have some kind of order and decency.

When you come to schools like this, they don't have no set order. When you don't have a set order, you just kinda lose your will to learn. Where if you went to a normal school that had more things than they wanted to teach you, it would be better for you.

Now, if I worked hard to do it, I want to know how come I couldn't get over there?

I wasn't sayin' blacks are dummies, because there is some smart people. Blacks is smart people. But even to the black smart people the white folks seem like they always get their opportunities first.

For instance, look who's in there for our president—Ronald Reagan. He's cuttin' everything down for the blacks. Blacks, blacks, blacks. The whites is over there gettin' the better things, which we should have too. We wanted Jesse Jackson in there. He's smart. But they wouldn't let him in there, now would they? He marched with Martin Luther King. He helped people with Coca Cola, remember when he was fighting against Coca Cola? And still, they don't even want him because of his race, they don't want to even give him a chance. Ronald Reagan was for a while tryin' to get a war started!

When kids drop out and things like that, it's not because of something's at home. It's when they come to school. Every place they go, it seems like this, "Well, shoot, everybody gettin' a better thing than I am, so why even care about it? I just might as well give it up and leave it alone."

When I tried to go to a better school, this is the way it went. I has signed up for a lot of courses to go to different schools. My cousin, she goes over to McKinley. She makes good grades. She ain't really poor and she kinda got it together. So I feel like this: Well, you've got a father who works and helps you. I can do it with just me and my mother. I have proved that I could get good as grades that she could, so that I could go up there to her same school in competition against her. And then they would give me encouragement and build up my ability to learn more.

But they still got me on the waitin' list and I was lookin' forward to goin' there. Not there was nothin' wrong with comin' down here. All schools have drugs and skippin' and things. They say, "Well, you want to do this? Okay, you do that. But you do it outside here. You do not come in this school and mess around." When you have places like that, I think that they seem to progress more. I like to go to a place like that, go around people who like to have fun without doing things and people talk about droppin' out, people comin' around pregnant, havin' drugs in all the schools here.

I have nieces and nephews. Okay? One niece, she's totally black. She knows things. She's no complete dummy. She knows things because her folks try to help her. But I have a nephew who's white. His father is up on education. He knows three times more as my little niece and that don't make no sense.

It just seem like the whites get their choice. Black people can't open their own business. But the white people, they always got their businesses. And black people always have to get jobs from them. The white man is always dishing out the money that they want to give to the black folks.

The white folks have power. They have things that we don't have. The white folks want their kids to learn and always be on top. That's the way it is. They want their kids to always say, "Well, because you're black, you goin' stay down here, and we goin' be up here." It's like that.

The Hangers-In

. . . I have a dream
That my four little children
Will one day live in a nation
Where they will not be judged
By the color of their skin
But by the content of their character.

—MARTIN LUTHER KING, Jr.

Noel, 16

"She goin' need me for somethin'. And I want to help."

The Hangers-In

My mother, she never care. When I was in junior high school I use to smoke weed. And I use to get us suspended every so and so. And when I get my report card and stuff, I'd still do good in school and stuff right? And I get my report card and she didn't even care about my report card. I'd say "Here's my report card" and all that stuff. I just didn't care about it and she didn't care about it. I just never talk to my mom.

Where does she live? I don't know. I think she got married again. I don't like 'em. I never really liked my mother that much, anyway. My dad's in New York. I always wanted to stay with my father. But when they went to court and got a divorce, I had to stay with her, instead.

I don't think I'm going to go to college. I'm going to complete high school, yeah. I'm going to get my high school diploma. You need that to get into the Air Force, anyway. So I'll go in the Air Force. I'll take a year off and go into the Air Force. Kick back and have a little job, have some money, get a car, something.

I'm goin' be somebody one day when I be havin' all this stuff. My mother goin' come back and ask for somethin'. She goin' need me for somethin'. And I want to help.

The Hangers-In

Maureen Manson, Grade 5
Maple Avenue School, Newark

School is important to me because I want to become somebody. I want to be able to go back to my teachers and tell them thank you. I want to be able to let my teacher see me on Divorce Court as a lawyer. I want to be able to get a job! I want to be able to get my own business. I want to get an education!

Katina, 13

*"None of my family never talks about college.
I'm the only oddball out of everybody."*

The Hangers-In

Most of my friends go to school, but I have some that dropped out. And I be telling them they have to go to school because back in other days people had to pay to get an education, and we got it free, so we better get it while we can. But some of them just want to get pregnant, get on with it.

They think they got it made, but they don't know when they go look for a job, they have to read the application. How they going to be able to fill it out? They gonna want some other friend that went to school to come and fill it out for them. That's not gonna be that way all the time.

Some of them dropped out because of family problems. Some of them dropped out because of the teachers. They didn't want to listen. They want to be their own boss. They don't want anybody telling them nothing. And some of them just dropped out because a boy tell them they love them and gonna keep on, and get a house. They gonna live—fancy cars, have kids—and they think it's true. But it's only a fantasy he's telling them. And he got her pregnant. Now she's sitting, because everybody knows that she's pregnant and had a baby. And they're just saying, "Well, look at her, she's a dropout and now she want to come back to school."

My friends, most of them, feel the same way as me because we be up bright and early. Some of us pick each other up. Only time we stay home is like we sick or we have a problem when we can't come to school. But other than that, we here.

When I was younger, at one time, I wanted to drop out because things weren't going right. A certain teacher I had, she didn't like me and I didn't like her. She's the type of teacher that have a lot of classes and stuff and, you know, you might get on her nerves but it's not right for her to take it out on our class. We haven't done anything to her. She be sitting, writing on the board, and we ask a question. She snaps at you. It be wrong, because I have a quick temper and she has a attitude, you know. It's just not right.

So when everybody come down on a kid, it's so much they can take. Everybody would dropout. Leave home, drop out, and go hang out. Be on the corner, sleep in abandoned buildings.

I was going to dropout but my best friend said if I dropped out I ain't going to be nothing, be like the rest of the kids on welfare—have babies—or not on welfare, walking around with dirty clothes on. And that's not me. So she told me to hang in then, everything will work out.

I don't ask my parents for much. I ask for money or certain things I don't understand. I go to my older sisters or brothers because they more like my age and they still in school.

The Hangers-In

They can show us the way they doin' it. My parents, they keep doin' it old-time way, you know. Like, "Well, we used to do it like this." And I don't have time for all that. If I don't understand a division problem, my mother goes, "Well, we used to do it like this" and such and such. She just be talkin' and talkin', and I already started doin' the answer to the problem.

Sometimes, when I have a problem with a boy, I'd go to my mother with it, though. With school work I'd rather go to my older sisters or brother. One is seventeen and one is fifteen. The one fifteen, me and her, we can get it off because she's about in the tenth grade now. I really go to her more because . . . she just left all this stuff I'm gettin' to do. She shows me how to do it.

Shifana, she seventeen. She thought of dropping out once. She moved to Ohio. She's down with her grandmother because her grandmother on her father's side got very sick. So she's down there. She thought about dropping out because she had a baby. She got pregnant, but she got an abortion while she was down there. She didn't know what to do because she didn't have my mother there. You know, she went ahead and had an abortion. And then, after that, that tore her apart because she didn't really want to have it. She wanted to drop out of school because all the problems and stuff and raising the baby.

So she called home. She told my mother she wasn't going back to school. So my mother went down to Ohio and I guess she cried it all out. And now she's back in school. It's her last year, gettin' her diploma, and she's ready to work. She have a job. Like we has some people that come here and talk to the eighth graders about school, and if you take up training, if you're good at it, you have a job when you get out. So when she get out, she'll be workin' right like that.

None of my family never talks about college. I'm the only odd ball out of everybody. Me and my little brother. I thought my oldest brother was going to go to college, but he went straight into the army.

My family is not so hot, really. Well, I put it to you like this. I have a crazy family, because they drink a lot and they want to fight each other. They don't want to listen. Everybody want to be top, nobody want to be small. And everybody gets in a fight. They just drink so much. I got an alcoholic family. Only time I like them is when they sober and they fun.

They know how to be happy, but if they get drunk, you have to be up at 2:30 A.M. and listen to them. And then in the morning time they just can be so sorry: "I'm so sorry, I didn't mean it."

I been wantin' to get out. I don't never stay home. I been in the street because I hate my house. I never want none of my friends to spend the night with me.

The Hangers-In

Last year, I used to have it bad because it used to mess me up. If it wasn't for Miss Brown, I wouldn't be in the eighth grade. See, I had a lot of problems on my mind. I couldn't do my work right. I wouldn't want to go to sleep and stuff. Like, I was a drug addict. But Miss Brown, she kept my spirit up.

Her and Mr. Brown tell me about a eagle story, how I had a dream that I wanted to be a teacher. They said you keep living with that dream, you'll make it. So here I am in the eighth grade, hoping to make it to the ninth.

If they don't shut up, I'm going to kill somebody in that house. My family, they aren't like others. They just drink too much. I stay downstairs. I have a two-family house. I stay on the first floor with my mother. It's all women in that house with their husbands and their girlfriends, and everybody want to do this at the same time and if one don't like it, they sang, 'cause they drunk.

We only have one sober person mind in that house and that's my Aunt Brenda. But she can't do much, because they don't want to listen. Everybody want to be the Indian and not no chief. I don't stay home. I be over to one of my friend's house. I sleep there, at my house. But I make sure I get real tired, enough so that when I go in the house I just go to sleep because I hate to be home.

Five years from now I will be in the army, takin' up a training. If I'm not in the army, I'll be sittin' back in my house, in my chair, watchin' TV. I was tellin' my mother about college but it don't seem exciting to me. They don't really fit with me. It's just like a roommate and classes. It's just like high school to me. You have to get a scholarship.

The army be better because it's more challenge. I like to get up early. I like to do things. I like to listen to other people. At ease! I like things like that. I just like it, that's all.

Am I going to make it to ninth grade? Oh, yeah. I put everything in mind. I'm going to make it.

The Hangers-In

I don't remember the name of the story,
but the hero, a boy, was lost,
wandering a labyrinth of caverns
filling stratum by stratum with water.

I was wondering what might happen:
would he float upward toward light?
Or would he somersault forever
in an underground black river?

I couldn't stop reading the book
because I had to know the answer,
because my mother was leaving again—
the lid of the trunk thrown open,

blouses torn from their hangers,
the crazy shouting among the rooms.
The boy found it impossible to see
which passage led to safety.

One yellow finger of flame
wavered on his last match.
There was a blur of perfume—
mother breaking miniature bottles,

then my father gripping her,
but too tightly, by both arms.
The boy wasn't able to breathe.
I think he wanted me to help,

but I was small, and it was late.
And my mother was sobbing now,
no longer cursing her life,
repeating my father's name

among bright islands of skirts
circling the rim of the bed.
I can't recall the whole story,
what happened at the end...

Sometimes I worry that the boy
is still searching below the earth
for a thin pencil of light,
that I can almost hear him

through great volumes of water,
through centuries of stone,
crying my name among blind fish
wanting so much to come home.

—"The Mystery of the Caves"
MICHAEL WATERS

Kisha, 16

"Parents, they always remember the bad things...
They don't realize that ain't helping you now.
You need somebody to say:
'Well, that was good what you did.' "

The Hangers-In

159

I got suspended in elementary school 'cause I had a fight. I got suspended in junior high for playin' in the hallway. I got suspended up here for not being in class. And each time I got suspended, my mom said, "Well, Kisha, you're supposed to be the good one. You not supposed to be suspended."

My brother, last year, he gets suspended. That's like nothin', 'cause she used to it. But me, it's like she all down my throat.

She want me to do so good. And it be hard tryin' to please her. I be doing my best, but you know, when you slip up and make a mistake, she right there. She notices. She knows and she be on my back.

As long as I do halfway good, I'd be satisfied with myself. I don't want to do bad. But if I don't make straight A's, it won't bother me as long as I know I've tried and I don't really mess up. My mom, she really look at the citizenship more than at scholarship. She said if I couldn't do the work, at least I know how to act. But my mom, she don't know I can do better. I just got to keep trying. But she look at the citizenship more 'cause she say, "At least know how to act in class."

Parents, they always remember the bad things. Really deep inside, they be trying to help you. They think if they keep throwing this stuff in your face, you're going to change. They don't realize that that ain't helping you now. You need somebody to say, "Well, that was good what you did." They're really tearing you down when they always throwing it in your face.

My brother, he was bad when he was at school. One of my older sisters, she was real bad when she was in school. Every time I do something bad, my mom stick it to me for everything. She always throw it in my face. She say, "Well, you goin' to turn out like them." Then when I do something good, she compliments me, but it's only for a little while. If I do something bad it stay with me forever. Me and my other sisters, we all right, we bad, but not like they do.

I can't get along with my stepfather. We used to fight all the time. I just couldn't stand him. I used to like him before him and my mother got married. That's why I'm living with my auntie now. Because we can't get along. Sometimes, I get mad at my mother. I want to be with her, but he's in the way. He's done her wrong, too. I be trying to tell her, just leave him alone. Let him go. He even told me he hated me, you know. My mom, she's in the middle and she don't know what to do because she loves him and she loves me. But we don't get along.

Are bad teachers an influence in dropping out? I think it is. Some people come here and don't nobody care about 'em already. So they already pushed off to the side. They can't do good in the classroom if the teacher is not helping them.

It's like, "Well, don't nobody else care 'bout me, so I'll care about myself. And if I drop out, it's all right. I'm just another person."

Some people they tryin' to help theirself. Some of 'em go to night school even though they dropped out. But other people, you know, they don't care. I feel sorry for 'em, because some of 'em really need somebody.

I hope I never drop out. I've got one more year. That's my last. I hope I don't drop out. Sometimes I be getting mad and I really get to the point where I tell myself I'm goin' drop out when stuff don't be goin' right.

Five years from now? I might be comin' out of college or comin' out of one of the armed forces. By that time, I want to be at least workin' as a counselor. As a group counselor or a child counselor. Then I want to start my studies as a psychologist.

I want to be happy in whatever I do. I got to prove to myself 'cause there's so much pressure on me to be somebody and do good. It seem like I'm goin' to slip somewhere. But I gotta keep on provin' to myself I can do somethin'. It's hard, though, because it's all that on me—all my sisters is older than me and my brothers. It's like, "Kisha, you goin' do good whether you want to or not."

And I know that I could do good and I feel I am. But you know, what if I just slip up and mess up?

The Hangers-In

Suppose you take a kid, and the teacher wants him in a certain way. The kid would be kinda mad and then the kid wouldn't act right at all. You have yourself a complete failure right there.

—Franklin, 12

Brian, 15

*"If you have a good teacher,
you want to go to school all the time."*

The Hangers-In

It's important to stay in school if you want to really get a job, get a good job. If you drop out of school, you know you workin' at McDonald's somewhere.

Certain people go to high school, get a diploma, get a limousine, Rolls Royce, graduate, work at Burger King. That's all they do. It's easy for me to go to high school because I'm big and everything. They want me to play football for the team. So it's easy for me and I like playing football.

I have a friend who dropped out. And he sells drugs. And he have problems. He just bought a car. He's like trying to tell me that, you know, you going to get out of school and work with him. I was thinking about it for a week. He's working and I play football, and he's getting mad and everything.

He said I not going to get caught.

"If you get caught, I get you out because I got money and everything," he said.

"Don't worry about it," he said.

But I told him no, I ain't gonna sell any drugs for him.

He dropped out of school and now he got kicked out of the apartment because his mother found out he sells drugs. And his mother went off on him and how he living in an abandoned building and is lookin' around for a house.

Now he feel sorry for himself. I feel sorry for him, though. He pick any different girl everyday. Different girl. He sell the crack stuff. He sell that, give it to her everyday. Every day different girl.

And these girls go crazy. And these girls, these days, as long as you got a car, they go with you. I'm serious. If you have a nice car, they go with you. A loud radio, they go with you. A girl told me, "If you have a car, I go with you." She told me. They tell you that. They tell you stuff like that. As long as you got a car, they go with you. They see you got some gold and stuff on you, they go with you.

I told my father what the boy said. My father said, "You do that, think what you gonna be in ten years from now."

I just think, "No, I won't do it."

He said, "You think he can be still selling drugs? They won't catch him?"

I say they gonna catch him. I play football.

My father tell me all this stuff he knows. Like he say, "Do your work" and all this stuff. When I first got into the gym, my father was sayin', "Okay, right now, if you start liftin' weights and stop all your school work, you going to be a dummy." You know, walkin' around the school, a big dummy. He's real big and he's not that dumb. So I said, "All right."

I got mad at him at first, but now I do what he say and everything. When I need help with my homework, I don't ask my father because he talks too much. My sister, she's real smart, she got skipped. She sixteen in the twelve grade. She goin' to UCLA. She went real fast, real smart.

If you have a good teacher, you want to go to school all the time. You know, like dropouts, I don't think it's the students' fault. They dumb. Some are dumb. Some have problems with the teacher. You were bad in one school and then the records put you as bad in everything you do. Then other teachers get the records redirected and they say this student is bad. Teachers say he bad and everything and treat the student real mean. Then he dropout.

Just like Marcus. His cousin, John is real bad and everything, but Marcus is not really bad. First day Marcus came to school, the teacher say, "Oh, my God, here is John's cousin.'

He set Marcus off. He shouldn't said that. And Marcus not a bad one, another John. Ever since he said that, Marcus is goin' crazy, not doin' the work, comin' to school, what, ten o'clock. Don't take off his coat, ten minutes to take it off. He's really messin', a lot of teachers be messin' up. Marcus, he dropped out, don't go to school no more.

Probably sell drugs now. He was a real nice person. The teacher shouldn't have said that.

Miss Jones is real nice. She take time with you. It mostly the teachers fault, the dropout, mostly the teacher's not students.

But some of these girls that get pregnant, these girls don't have to be nice. They always say it's the boys fault. It's not the boys fault. Some boys will do it anyway. So, you don't have to. You can say "no" instead of "yeah, okay." I don't feel sorry for none of these girls. It's their fault. It's not the boy's fault. You know the boy is gonna do it. If I had a girl always talked to me and stuff, I'd say, "No." But it's the girl's fault. I don't feel sorry for none of them. They go around with their welfare. I'd laugh in their face. That's your problem. She shouldn't did it.

It wouldn't be my baby. My sister wouldn't do anything like that. My sister's already got her career. She just won a pageant. She goin' to California.

I stayed back in the third grade and another grade. I stayed back because I was playin' all the time. I felt like droppin' out then. I was gettin F's and D's and all that stuff. But now I'm fifteen in the eighth grade, so now I'm getting all A's and B's. We just took a test, a math test, last week and I has one of the highest scores in the whole school. Everybody failed. I passed the test. And I don't even like math. I can't stand that.

People like me, but I don't know why. Some people just don't like me. They're sayin' because you're big and you can do all this stuff. Because you're big don't mean you can do that. People say that must be jealous. Actually, this girl, she didn't even like me 'til I started lifting weights. I came to school this year. They all be around me because I be in magazines. You know, weight liftin' magazines? I be in there on a stage, liftin' all this stuff.

A lot of my teachers used to say, "Never be a failure, be the best you can be." It's been with me since fourth grade on up. Do I think I'm going to make it to the ninth grade? Yeah, positive about that. I got this far.

The Hangers-In

168

Mention a word,
just the word,
a word I can't say too loud.
(It doesn't deserve it.)
The word is math.
When Mrs. Sorkin
says math time,
the ocean,
the roaring ocean
that got sand in my hair
last summer,
when she says math,
like having itchy sand all over,
makes me feel that my
life is going to end.

—KATHY BERENSON, 9

Part Five

The Beginners,
The Principal, The Teacher
and The Young Bronx
Entrepreneurs

The elementary school kids were so bright and motivated and interested, and they had so much hope and so many ambitions, that it was impossible to imagine them as ever becoming disheartened or aimless. They talked about passionate teachers and dreamed of the day when they would reward their teachers and parents by their accomplishments. Their dreams were effervescent and plentiful: they were going to be policemen, firemen, lawyers, nurses, doctors, basketball players, college professors. "I love school," one said. "I live for school."

Coleman Brown was among the spunkiest and most self-possessed at the Border Star Elementary School in Dallas. What he says parallels much of what his peers had to say. Asked by CHILDREN'S EXPRESS who she admired, Tina, Coleman's ten-year-old classmate, said, "Well, nobody really impresses me. I impress myself." These kids possessed a self-confidence that was rarely seen among the teenagers.

We interviewed dozens of adults—academicians, teachers, administrators, businessmen—who were invaluable in the preparation of the book. We decided, however, not to bring in the "adult filter" by using their interviews directly. Two exceptions were Roberto Marquis, principal of Sunset High School in Dallas, and Steve Mariotti, the South Bronx's pied piper of private enterprise.

Marquis is a dropout who not only made good, but returned to school as a professional uniquely qualified to understand what drives children from school. Mariotti, a former Ford Motor Company executive, turned a personal disaster into a fruitful mission, transforming lives in one of the nation's bleakest neighborhoods by teaching high school students the basics of self-employment. Howard Stubbs, the seventeen-year-old hot dog man, is one of the many proofs of the promise in Mariotti's method. It seems to be no coincidence that among Howard's dreams is the desire to return one day and help other disadvantaged kids.

Teen Editors: *Glenn Golz*
                Jonathan Zachary

Coleman, 11

*"If you don't have an education,
you wouldn't be nothin' in life."*

The Beginners

My name is Coleman Brown. I'm eleven years old. I have one brother and one sister. My life is mostly terrific. I get to do other things than some children, like going to play basketball and baseball and fool around and doing things.

I go to the Border Star Elementary School and I'm in the sixth grade. My teacher's name is Mr. McIntyre. My principal's name is Ms. Kirksey. I think that it's a good school because of the teachers. They get you learnin' things faster than other schools. When you're in the sixth grade, you have to be ready for all those big exams an' tests for junior high school.

You learn how to do artistic things. You learn how to read and write and you also learn how to pick up things fast. And teachers, they help you. They're passionate with you.

When you start having trouble in your subjects, you can ask the teacher to help you and she'll help you. All of my teachers were good teachers. They taught me a lot through the school year. And they helped me with falling behind.

I'd describe myself as an A-plus student. Some people might not say that, but that's how I would describe myself. Most of the time I be obedient. I listen to what the teacher says. Off and on, I kinda slip with my mouth. Like talk. I don't talk to get in trouble. I talk just to know what's goin' on, like, "Did you watch that pitcher last night?" And then the teacher would say, "Be quiet."

I understand my work and get most of it correct. Sam don't finish his work. And he believes like you don't have to finish work, get your assignments done at the right date. And all his stuff has been late, so he may not graduate. And he tells stories to the teacher like when the teacher asked him to do something, he takes something from the teacher. He takes the teacher's markers and he say no. Everybody else know what they did and he tell lies. I feel he's making a terrible mistake. He does it to get attention. Because he's probably not learning as much as he thought he would.

See, like in the sixth grade, we learn a lot so you can go to the seventh. He might feel he's not gettin' enough education and he's not learning as much as he should. Because most of the time, when the teacher say any questions, he don't speak up. He don't get 'em right, get the answers right.

I have to find my abilities and I have to do my work because if you don't get good grades you're not going to pass to the next grade. If you don't want to do well, you might as well say you should just drop out.

The Beginners

Some people don't think that school is very important and they're doing something that they don't have to do. So they drop out. A dropout is a person that don't want to learn anything and a person who is thick-headed and a person who think they know it all. But they don't know nothin'.

I want to finish school and go to a private college. If I dropped out my parents would be shocked. Because I dropped out when I wasn't even close to, really close to finishing school. They would feel disappointed because I came this far and why should I stop. They would feel like I should move away from my parents because I dropped out school and I don't have a job and a school education.

School is important because you have to have an education in order to be able to get a good job. So you can be something in life. Because if you don't have an education, you wouldn't be nothin' in life.

CE: What's your goal?
COLEMAN: To get out of school.

CE: If you had a friend who wanted to drop out, what would you tell him?
COLEMAN; I would tell him to get on about his business.

CE: What do you mean?
COLEMAN: Like, see, they might want me to drop out of school and I don't want to
    drop out of school. That isn't the right thing to do. 'Cause you should try to get
    an education while you can. People drop out of school because they don't wanna
    learn their skills and they don't wanna learn how to obey the teachers and they
    don't wanna get a job. I feel that an education is free. So you shouldn't drop out
    of school. You should try to get your education while you can.

CE: Do you think having a bad teacher can make someone want to drop out of school?
COLEMAN: Yep. Because if they have a bad teacher that's always grouchy at them, then
    they wouldn't want to be in their class.

CE: What if you got a really bad teacher? What would you do?
COLEMAN: I would just try to make the best of it.

CE: If someone said to you, Coleman, take your school and make some serious changes
    to make it the best school in the country. What would you do to improve it?
COLEMAN: I would make it have more hours and make the school last a little longer
    and make them teach you more.

CE: How long does it last now?
COLEMAN: School lasts for nine months. And while you're at school, it lasts six hours.
    I would want it to last for, oh, about nine. So that you can get mostly 'bout ten
    pages of everything done instead of 'bout like four or five a day.

CE: Wouldn't you get tired doing nine hours of school?

COLEMAN: Not really, 'cause you'll be gettin' a free education.

CE: But you're getting a free education now. How would other students feel if the school hours were changed to nine?

COLEMAN: They would probably want to drop out.

CE: So what do you think? Do you still want to do that even if it would make kids want to drop out?

COLEMAN: Sort of.

CE: Why?

COLEMAN: Because you'll learn a little more.

The Beginners

178

Where the bee sucks, there suck I
In a cowslip's bell I lie;
There I couch when owls do cry.
On the bat's back I do fly
After summer merrily:
Merrily, merrily shall I live now
Under the blossom that hangs on the bough.

—The Tempest
WILLIAM SHAKESPEARE

The Beginners

179

Ce Mira Gamble, Grade 4
Maple Avenue School, Newark

If I were principal I would make a lot of changes. I would keep water in all the sinks, keep the playground clean, keep the school clean, and have all the supplies the school needs. I would talk with teachers, and on a cold day I would also have heat in the school. I would make sure that anyone who doesn't belong here does not come in school. I will speak on a speaker. I will work at the school and work until I'm fifty-six.

Roberto Marquis,

Principal

Sunset High School,

Dallas

*"There's a misconception that kids that drop out
of high school are not intelligent.
They're some of the most intelligent."*

The Principal

What's the best and worst about being a principal? I never think about the worst parts because they'll wear you down. The only thing I ever think about is the good parts and that's being around the kids more than anything else. I like to be around kids.

I'm a high school dropout. The way we try to handle problems is on an individual basis. I don't like treating human beings in groups. They lose their identity, then you have a problem with that kid. We try to individualize it to where we deal with them one-on-one and not punish an entire group for the sins of a few, but deal with those few as individuals.

I can't take these kids home. I don't have control over them when they leave this building. I can't change their lives outside. The only thing we can do is when they walk in the front door of this school, we have a consistency here.

We have a set of rules and a set of expectations. Everybody is treated equally. Everybody is dealt with in the same way. We don't make allowances for one individual that we don't make for others. The kids know that there's a place in their lives that they can go where the same faces and the same people and the same things are always going to be there.

Out there, things change for them day in and day out. One third of our kids move every year. I doubt if ten percent of the kids that start here as freshman actually wind up graduating from this school. Nobody knows where they go. All we know is that they come through and they're gone one year to the next. But the thing that school can do that's more important than anything else is to be consistent. That's it. It provides the only consistency in the kid's life.

Why did I drop out? I didn't see any need in going to school. I didn't project myself going to college. Somebody said to me all along the way, "Well, you're one of eleven kids. You're not going to college."

My dad raised eleven kids and he never went to college. He never graduated from high school. I didn't see any need in graduating from high school 'cause I could go to work and make as much money, if not more than my dad would ever make. I could see myself buying a house right down the street from where my parents grew up.

I already had my life figured out when I was a kid. I said, "Well, what's the sense of wasting my time going to school when I can just go out there and go to work."

There's a misconception that kids that drop out of high school are not intelligent. They're some of the most intelligent. Sometimes they don't pay attention in class because they're smart alecks and already know it.

I used to have a teacher who gave me multiple choice history test. I'd skip school all the time. I'd come in on Fridays and take her test and I'd make an A. I already knew it. She used to put me in another teacher's class who was off that period. That teacher's job was to watch me take the test, to see to it that I didn't cheat. They couldn't figure out how I was doing it.

It's kind of like, you know, you defy the system. There's a way to defy the system in any way, shape or form. You can defy it passively or you can defy it overtly. The passive resistant kids are the ones that drive everybody crazy. The overt kid—he's easy to deal with. The kid that disrupts and the kid that wrecks your class —you can get rid of him in a minute, bam!

The one that really hurts you, that will drive teachers up the wall, is the passive kid. The smart, passive kid who walks in every so often, who sits there and just looks at you and will not do a darn thing, that kid blows your consistency in the classrooms. He doesn't see any reason for being in the school.

One of the things we do more and more, day in and day out, is motivate. It's the one thing I think we try to do more than anyone else. I have seventeen hundred kids here. How many kids do I reach? It's so different for every human being. A lot of time kids say, "Well, nobody motivated me." That's not true. Somebody tried.

Very few kids ever go through school without a teacher or some adult saying, "Hey, you can do better." Or, "That was very good," or "You did a great job." But they don't have it often enough. The schools can't cover every aspect of it. That's what parents were designed to do. That's the whole idea of having kids, for someone to be at home to say, "Hey, you're a great human being. You're a fine young man and I'm proud of you."

We can do it. But the kids look at us here at school and they say, "Well, you people get paid to say things like that."

We don't get paid to do that. We get paid to do very little. But we do a heck of a lot for kids.

Our attitude has to remain constant. That's the funny thing about it. You see, you can evolve as a person, you can change, but your basic premise of engineering this job always has to be the same. If you ever lose that, then you need to leave, because that's what keeps you doing your job. My whole basic reason for entering the teaching profession was to help kids. I keep that in the forefront. The day I forget it, that's the day all those bad things I told you I don't like talking about, they creep up on you and close in on you. Then you lose your whole impact, your whole perspective.

My impact upon kids is good because I remember that the one reason I'm here—the only reason I'm here—is to serve them. That's all I have in my life. Without that I'll be some crusty old administrator who sits behind his desk and shuffles his papers all day.

The Principal

Why do I want to help them? All of us, I think, want to save the world and make it a better place.

One thing I always tell the teachers is that we can't blame the kids because the good Lord gave them the parents He gave them. And the only thing that we can do is take care of the kids and try to make them good human beings.

I had an eighteen-year-old arrested before I left this morning to go to my meeting. They had a problem outside the school and this girl came up on campus to beat up some sixteen-year-old because they had a problem three months ago, somewhere out there.

See? They bring all that excess baggage. But you see, the school has to say, "This is school, and school is different. Schools have rules and schools care and schools demand and schools expect."

Are the rules here strict? It depends on who you talk to. If you talk to me, I'd say they're about as strict as I like having them. If you talk to somebody else, they'd say they could be stricter.

One of the worst things you can do for kids or anybody is create a system of dual standards. It's divisive. We never kick a kid out for tardiness. We're never going to kick a kid out for those kinds of things. We have an elaborate process that goes from dealing with them in the office to parent conference, to a series of hearings, and then recommendations for an alternative placement after that.

And expulsion is a rarity. If it would ever be used, it would be in an extremely severe case, an assault on a teacher or another student. That's why I had her sent to jail.

When an individual comes with that malice aforethought, then that's assault, and that's when you treat it differently.

But, no, kids aren't kicked out of school.

You don't kick out the lower spectrum of the school. What you find out is the kid that violates the system sometimes can be one of your smartest kids. If we were to give IQ tests to a lot of our kids who come and go and play the silly game of cutting class, that would get to us. That's what drives us crazy sometimes. Because they won't come. See, they're so smart that they actually, legitimately think they're smarter than the system and have all the answers.

That's the way I used to feel. I used to feel I could beat the system, like I was smarter than people in the system. What I realized was that I couldn't go on beating the system forever. The only way to ever change the system is to do it from within.

I think that administrators in positions like mine have all forgotten that the key reason for them being there is to serve the kids, not vice versa. Everybody has got the kids serving the teachers and the administrators. And it's the other way around.

The Principal

186

What's happened is everybody's forgotten. We've set up schools for adults, not kids. You don't have to change anything in the school except the attitude, to an attitude that says kids can do it.

Because if you ever think they can't, then what you've done, psychologically, is closed the door on that kid. You always have to think that no matter how tough they are, how poor they are, how difficult they are, and everything else, that they can do it—if you just expect them to.

The Principal

187

Shariek Scott, Grade 4
Maple Avenue School, Newark

If I was a principal I would be in my office doing my work and if kids would be bad I would give them another chance. If the kids would be bad again I would kick them out of school for two months. When they come back with their parents I would let them back in school. When I let the student back in school she or he will be well from now until June. If he or she passes I will be so happy that I might put them in their right school, that's in Weequahic School where they will be better off. When I send them there they will be so happy that they can't stop talking.

Steve Mariotti,

Teacher

*"The beauty of self-employment is that
it provides an immediate vision."*

The Teacher

I'm from the Midwest. I have an MBA, went to the University of Michigan. I worked at the Ford Motor Company for three years as a lower level executive. And then I started my own business, a relatively successful import-export business on the Lower East Side of New York. Then one night I went out and I got beaten up pretty severely. It traumatized me for about three or four months. I had some very painful flashbacks, to the point where I had difficulty walking down the street.

I was very angry with the kids that had beaten me up, who were young black and Hispanic youths. I understand people like Bernard Goetz, that flip out from that experience. If I had not gotten warm professional help from a psychologist who's a specialist in working through traumas, I would probably have ended up being a very bigoted, angry person for a long, long time, if not forever.

My parents were school teachers. I never wanted to be a teacher when I was a kid. It never occured to me I'd end up doing this. But it's a strange place, this world. I only planned when I first went into it to be there three or four months, just as a way of getting over this event, as a way of working off that trauma.

The first day I went into the school, I had a lot of anxiety. It was Maxwell Vocational High School in East New York, which is a very intense neighborhood. I felt like I could barely do it.

But once I got there, I realized everything was going to be all right. And by the end of the day I was totally over my trauma. I realized within the first two or three days that I found work that I really liked to do. And I'm going to do this the rest of my life. I knew right then that I found something that I was relatively good at and I believed in, and that made me feel like a hero every day.

I was a high school teacher of business for four years. During that time I realized that business education in the public school system was pretty much learning to type. I wanted to get kids more involved in starting their own businesses, or entrepreneurship.

Business at the high school level is almost always typing, particularly in the inner city. The kids in the suburbs, middle class white kids will get Junior Achievement. And they'll get a more expanded curriculum.

But in the inner cities, as far as I can see, when they say they're going to teach a kid business, it basically means typing and shorthand. It's aimed at the girls. The boys have nothing or very little.

I was at ten different schools and there was great resistance intellectually toward getting inner city black and Hispanic children involved in starting, financing and managing a small business. I was asked to leave seven or eight schools. I didn't really fit into the system the way it was.

The common argument was, "Well, they're behind in reading, math, and writing, how could they possibly run a small company?"

It was always my thought that they were putting it backwards, that the way to improve basic skills was to get them involved in something they were interested in. You've got to give them a vision. And the beauty of self-employment is that it provides an immediate vision.

Really, the only thing I knew anything about was small business, being an entrepreneur. So I began to teach that. And I got very dramatic results, immediately. I got a lot of positive feedback from the children. My kids would stay in school much longer and made some improvement in math and reading.

That gave me the idea that maybe entrepreneurship was of great interest to inner city kids, that there was a fit there. I'm very proud of the fact that every child I've had during the past two and a half years has learned, has been required to form some type of sole proprietorship.

Only one in every twenty-five Americans ever begins their own company, sole proprietorship, corporation or partnership. A vast majority of people never try self-employment. I think we're making a big mistake by starting in high school. I think we should be starting in kindergarten, first, second grade, so that everybody knows the basics of self-employment.

We've been very successful. We've started seventy-eight small companies. I think sixty-four of them are owned and operated by black and Hispanic youths between fourteen and eighteen. Total sales are now over $80,000. An average kid has about $900 of sales a year, which isn't very much, but it's not what they're doing now that's important. It's what they're doing twenty years from now.

I had my first two assignments in Bedford Stuyvesant and East New York, where a significant portion of the kids were black and Hispanic. I'd go there and ask for kids that were highly at risk. I found that a lot of young men were dropping out of school and were psychologically alienated from the system.

A lot of these kids, they've got no chance other than self-employment. For a wide variety of reasons many inner city young men have difficulty fitting into bureaucracies and into a structured environment. And that's nothing to be ashamed of. Many times that's a blessing. Henry Ford, Billy Durant, some of our greatest businessmen of all time were like that too.

A lot of these kids have behavior problems or they're rude or they're angry. They're not bad people. They just don't have a vision. I really believe that every kid is a wonderful human being and that, if guided correctly, will be a very positive force in our society.

I think we should have a crash program (of self-employment) in the inner cities, where it's a matter of life and death. One in every twenty black male teenagers is murdered between the ages of thirteen and twenty. These kids are packed into these projects where every single day of their lives it's a wartime situation in the sense you've got to worry about your sister getting raped, you getting robbed. You can't accumulate capital. If you start to do well and accumulate capital, there's a good chance you're going to get mugged, beaten or murdered.

We're dealing here not with a research paper. We're dealing with what I think is an emergency situation. And I believe that every single kid entering the school system should learn the basics of self-employment by fourth grade.

You can raise a kid's math level from first or second grade to seventh or eighth grade in three months. They learn how to read. I had a little girl that learned how to read from the Avon book in three campaigns, in six weeks. She was defined as being dyslexic and people had given up on her. She was seventeen years old. She became the youngest Avon rep in New York City. Her first campaign netted her $336 in sales. And, by God, she just sat down and said, "I'm going to learn how to read."

A big problem in the inner city is that about half of the women get pregnant before they turn twenty. And about half of those that get pregnant have the baby. So you've got one in four women having babies before they're twenty, and most of those babies are born out of wedlock.

I found that my girls are much less likely to have unplanned pregnancies because giving birth to a business kind of takes the place of having to give birth to a baby. You can give love and attention to the business. And that's a major finding, one of the most important findings in social sciences in the past ten years.

One of the reasons for poverty in ghetto areas—Bedford Stuyvesant, Harlem, East New York, South Bronx, Watts, Chicago's South Side—is because the native sons of those communities are left out of the distribution system.

The goods come in from Southeast Asia. They go to the docks. They go to either the Lower East Side of New York or up to Thirtieth Street and Broadway. From there they go to white merchants. So a big focus of our work is teaching kids the concept of manufacturing, wholesale and distribution.

There was a lot of resistance to having groups of four or five young black men and women come into a wholesale shop. We were actually locked out of wholesale places.

On several occasions we were treated very rudely. Angry words were exchanged. And I'd remind myself that I was in America.

By constantly working on it, we found nine wholesalers that are now very enthused about our program and are working directly with these kids.

All of the children that I've worked with have had almost a zero net worth. Most of the kids have no money when they begin. The Trickle Up Program, one of the most dynamic and successful anti-poverty programs I'm aware of, gives fifty dollars to any kid that wants to start a business. In three months if the young adult is still in business, he gets another fifty dollars. Then we give some money from my foundation. We get them business cards. We get them ads. We put them through a twenty-four hour training course. And then I constantly stay in touch with them.

All the businesses we've started have been on no capital. We try to demystify business. If you ask people about their dreams, they say, "Well, I'd like to be in business but I don't have enough money."

That's really a misconception. If you look at the history of American business, all the major companies have been started by people that at one time or another were broke. Henry Ford went bankrupt twice. Hershey went bankrupt twice. Billy Durant, who founded General Motors, went bankrupt three times. Capital's not the most important thing. It's the ideas in the mind.

As far as sales, I teach it by the same method that I used to overcome my trauma, the beating, with a concept called flooding. Most people are afraid to sell, so I just have them jump right in, like learning to swim.

The second week every kid has to make five mock sales calls during the day. And each kid also has to make two of those to me. And it can't be in the classroom. So they find all sorts of ingenious ways to hunt me down and make the sales call, including in the teacher's bathroom.

The vast majority of these kids are incredible, with just unlimited potential. We've got to start tapping that potential. Because of the conditions under which these kids grow up, they develop special characteristics. It's like God gives them this great tragedy of being born into a wartime situation, of being born into a society that is subliminally racist, and of having a lot of other obstacles. But the benefit is that they become mentally strong. They develop a finesse and a toughness to them, all the characteristics of the great entrepreneurs. If we play on that positive thing and pull on it, I think we can start to turn the inner cities around.

These kids are very honest people. And they have a great kindness I think that comes from suffering. The suffering either destroys you or makes you a better person.

Character is destiny. These kids are born entrepreneurs. I try to look at it as if these kids have a special ability. We should look at them as gifted in this field.

I don't like to say they're disadvantaged. I like to say that they have a new opportunity. Any kid that can get to be seventeen living in Forest Projects or McKinley Projects in the South Bronx—and live through it—is a remarkable human being.

Josephine, 17

Student, Mother, and

South Bronx Entrepreneur

CE: What do you do?

JOSEPHINE: Sell lingerie. Teddies, nightgowns, panties, garters. This year we made $10,000. We do flea markets and parties.

CE: How do you handle school along with a baby and a business?

JOSEPHINE: It's tough.

CE: What was school like before you started?

JOSEPHINE: Well, for a year I messed up in school.

CE: Why'd you mess up?

JOSEPHINE: Family problems.

CE: Has your business helped you with your reading and your math?

JOSEPHINE: Yes, a whole lot. You have to deal with numbers. Can't give away your profits. You have to write down the sales that you make. You have to give out receipts.

CE: What has your business taught you?

JOSEPHINE: Don't give up when you feel down.

Howard Stubbs, 17

South Bronx Entrepreneur

"I just got a four-year scholarship . . .
a $44,000 scholarship.
And I'm proud of it."

CE: What do you do?

HOWARD: I sell hot dogs.

CE: How did you start?

HOWARD: Well, my mother, she just finished college and couldn't get a job. She said, "You know, Howard, I have a friend that's in the hot dog business, has a hot dog cart, and she wants me to buy her own."

I said, "What, are you crazy? My mother selling hot dogs! You know what my friends are going to say?"

They all laughed when they heard and saw me pushing the hot dog cart. It was like, "Howard, what are you doing? You're working for somebody or something?"

I said, "No, this is my own."

They died laughing. I felt ashamed of it. But after the first day I was really, you know, so happy. I was like, "Wow!" What she made in that day, she would make in a week in one of her jobs, and it was great.

CE: Why hot dogs?

HOWARD: It just happened. My mother was just desperate and she had to do something at the moment or things would just go down the drain.

CE: How do you spend the money that you make?

HOWARD: On clothing, on girls, on more supplies, and I save some of it.

CE: What are you saving it for?

HOWARD: College. I'm saving it for college and to start my own business in the future. Because if I start now, saving, I put in my mind if I save at least a hundred dollars a week or two hundred dollars a week, you know, by the time I'm twenty, I can start my own little business. I want to really open a restaurant, then get into real estate after I make a lot of money.

CE: So, do you make enough?

HOWARD: Yeah. For a seventeen-year-old living in the Bronx, it's plenty.

CE: Are you saving up enough to start your own business or to go college?

HOWARD: Definitely. Definitely. The funny thing with that is I just got a four-year scholarship to Johnson & Wells, and it's a $44,000 scholarship. I'm real proud of it. And if I go through with that, I'll be selling hot dogs and making that profit and putting it all in the bank. So when I get out of college maybe I can open a little restaurant of my own.

CE: What training have you had in selling hot dogs?

HOWARD: Well, it all started when I was a young boy with my mother teaching me manners. She always told me, "Howard, manners maketh a man," and "If you treat people well, treat people good, no matter what race, creed or color, they'll treat you well."

Even with people that come up...say, real mean, "Give me a hot dog," I go, "What would you like on it, sir?" You know, I show them that they can be above just being grumpy and snotty, and they can be nice.

So the next time they come to me, they'll say, "Hey, you know, that guy was really nice to me. And they bring back other customers. And that's how I kind of make more business for myself.

CE: How do you handle school along with business?

HOWARD: I study a lot. And I do my homework, of course, for Monday through Friday. Then on the weekends, Saturday and Sunday, I work with my stand.

CE: What did you do before Howard's Hot Dogs?

HOWARD: Well, at the age of eight, I packed bags. My mother taught me how to pack bags, and I did really well for a little guy. I was always short. I had to stand on a crate, you know. I'd be standing on the crate, packing bags and saying, "Thank you" to the people. I used to make like eighty dollars a week packing bags.

After that, I went into summer youth program. And I worked with the elderly people, senior citizens. Then from there I was at my brother's college, Westminster Choir College, and I washed dishes. Then my mother got into the hot dog business.

CE: How was school going before the hot dog business?

HOWARD: Okay. I was never—I'm not a real good student. I'm not top A student. But you know, I hold my own. I try to get my nineties and eighties. But I'm doing the best I can. I'm still doing the same, so nothing is being messed up with school. If my schoolwork goes down, I stop for a week and I study. If I have a test, I have to study on the weekends. I don't work. School is first all the time.

CE: Has your hot dog selling helped you with your academics, reading and math and stuff?

HOWARD: To a certain extent, yes. Because when you go down to the wholesalers, right, you have to deal with numbers. A lot of time I would go and buy a hundred or two-hundred dollars worth of supplies, and he would ring me out for a hundred and ten, and I'd say, "That's wrong." I got one-hundred-one and ninety-five cents. We'd both have to go around and check our math and see. So that's like the mathematical thing about it. And plus you have to know how much profits you make, you have to check your books. And dealing with taxes—that's another form of math.

And reading the tax form is another form of reading and English. So that's kind of helped me also.

CE: What has your business taught you?

HOWARD: How to be a man. How to stand on my own two feet. That I can do anything I want to do as long as I have a goal and I have a vision, and if I think about it hard enough and act. And that's what mom taught me.

CE: What do your friends think about you selling hot dogs?

HOWARD: At first they laughed at me. They said, "Howard, the hot dog man." And to tell you the truth, at first I felt bad. I was like, man, you know, I really don't want to do this. And then at the end of every day, I'd have money in my pocket. I'd go, "I want to do this more! I want to do this tomorrow!"

I have the drive, the adrenalin. I'd get up the block and they'd say, "What's up, hot dog man?"

"What's up, frankfurter?"

They make their little jokes. And I go, "Oh, so what? I have money in my pocket."

Some of them are selling drugs. Some of them are doing drugs. I mean, they're not my personal friends, but even my personal friends made fun of me. But they saw that I was excelling, and now they can appreceiate it even more.

When I don't work, they all say, "Howard, why you didn't work today? What happened?" You know, they're concerned why I didn't go to work—not that I am working, but why didn't I go to work.

CE: Has Mr. Mariotti influenced you?

HOWARD: Well, he influenced me. I didn't know anything about taxes. I mean, I knew taxes were around and everything, that people had to pay, but I thought I had my license, I pay a tax on the food right there when I buy it, and that's all I thought. I didn't know I had to pay taxes every three months.

He's just recently said, "Howard, come on, you have to get on the ball."

I had to pay all my taxes and get all that out of the way. He's been a support to me. He's like a big brother. He calls me at night, calls me in the morning, sees how I'm doing, see if I'm still alive, you know what I mean? And he gets me a lot of publicity, and gets me a lot of people that's interested in me.

CE: How has he helped you?

HOWARD: He has built up my character. Sometimes he says, "Howard, I want you to give a speech."

And I freeze. I go like, "Oh, I don't want to do this."

He goes, "It's a piece of cake, Howard. Just go up there and tell them what you know."

And that has made me a better person and a better man. You know, I can go up there and stand up and talk to five hundred people and not sweat anymore. You know, I can really do that. Sometimes it amazes me. I kind of have fun with the crowd, like I just know them.

CE: And what has he taught you?

HOWARD: He's taught me bookkeeping and accounting. He's taught me how to write a business plan. He's taught me how to save my money and be smart. And that all the fifty dollar sneakers and all the fifty dollar shoes and hundred dollar this and hundred dollar that to buy, you know, he's . . . calmed me down. You know I like to dress up and go to clubs and stuff. He's kind of restrained that from me. Taken it away. But it's not really taken away. He's just making me see that I can save that money and do something better with it.

CE: There are kids that are on the street, you know, as old as you, selling drugs, that make a whole lot more than you. Does that bother you?

HOWARD: No, not really. Because they can't go home and look at their mother and go, "Mom, I made five hundred today." And then she says, "How did you make it?" And then you're saying, "I made it by killing someone."

You know what I mean? What am I doing? I'm feeding your stomach.

I feel proud when I go out there and push out my little hot dog stand. You know, I feel like a real business person, a businessman. I say, "This is my little corporation, this is my little store." You know, no matter what anyone would say, I'll have my hot dog stand and be proud.

But even my friends, some of them are selling drugs. And I say, "You know, we grew up together. Why do you have to go that way?"

He said, "Well, Howard, we're different. 'Cause you've had your training as a young man. Your training is different from my training, and my growing up is different from your growing up."

"Where you had a mother," he said. "I didn't have a mother. Where you had a father—he wasn't always there, but he'd call you. My father, I don't even know him."

So, when I get older, what I'm going to try to do is help those kids that don't have parents. All they have—I mean, what are they going to turn to? They can't read. And they haven't had the right amount of schooling, and no one has taught them. So you know, you can't really down them because they don't know anything else to do, you know?

The Entrepreneurs

Dropout Is Not The Word

Dropout is not the word
Dropout is not the word
Say it again,
Dropout is not the word

Stay in school, Mariotti,
He told me,
To be great, be magnificent
In everything you do.

Because
Dropout is not the word.
That's good.

—Vince Wilkins, 17
South Bronx Entrepreneur

Afterword

I had read many statistics, but nothing I had ever read prepared me for what I actually saw when I stepped into a Boston public high school for the first time. "There's a kid over there tied up in a strait jacket!" I gasped.

My astonishment turned to embarrassment as someone explained that the student was dressed for Halloween. I took this first experience as a warning about allowing my pre-conceived notions to interfere, though it wouldn't be the last assumption to fall by the wayside during the work on this project.

In our journey into the schools of America, we discovered that we were looking at a societal rather than an educational problem. Until you experience it, it's hard to believe it's that bad. There's such a great combination of problems, you begin to realize that these kids are caught in a community and a culture and a system. And you begin to recognize that there's no exit for these kids unless you can change their families and their communities.

One of the most interesting things we noticed was the definite attitudes each age level seemed to have concerning the role of school in their futures. Fourth and fifth graders liked school and said they couldn't wait to graduate from high school so that they could go on and become doctors and lawyers. Kids in the middle schools seemed less positive about their futures. Most of them just hoped that they could make it through high school and get jobs that paid a decent wage. For many high schoolers, school was nothing but a formality, unfairly imposed upon them by society.

Our standards for success in school changed dramatically while working on this book. The grades students get no longer seem so important. Whether they make it to tenth grade is.

When kids get no support from their parents, when they go through what so many of these kids go through, how can school be a priority? It's hard enough to be motivated at school when you don't have all these problems in your life.

How is a kid going to do her homework when she has no desk? How is he going to worry about history or math when he's worried about getting beaten up by a parent when he gets home? How is she going to concentrate on what the teacher is saying when she is starving for breakfast or lunch? What's a kid—when he's nine or ten or eleven years old—supposed to do when he's got drugs all over the place? What can you expect of a nine-year-old who's already expected to come home and cook dinner for himself and his younger brother?

Afterword

We found it unsettling to realize to what extent success in school is dependent upon the luck of which family a child is born into. So many of these kids were really smart and articulate. It's unfair to say to these kids, "Here is the playing field and these are the rules," and expect them to compete with both feet tied. And we were fascinated that despite the obstacles, some of these kids had so much drive.

We came to the conclusion that the causes of the dropout crisis are not educational in nature, but societal and multi-faceted. There is only so much a teacher can do. They can't all be therapists.

At times, reflecting on all we saw and heard, we felt hopeless about the possibility of changing the prospects for these kids or the younger ones who will come along to take their place.

Most of the teenagers we talked with said they had never had a chance to talk like this about their problems. They said that hearing they were not alone helped them, and they wanted to have more opportunities to talk like this.

The experience of working on this book transformed me into an ardent writer as well as a loyal child advocate. I couldn't get these kids and my feeling of responsibility for them out of my head. The idea of an inner city/suburban exchange consumed me.

If priveleged Marblehead students frequently ran exchanges with such far-off places as France, Spain and Russia, why shouldn't they have the opportunity to go live in Boston's inner-city neighborhood, Roxbury? It was only sixteen miles away and it was as foreign to me as any of the others.

Hours of meetings, telephone calls, photocopying and word processing, lack of sleep, microplasmic pneumonia and the fear of failure followed. But working with inner-city (METCO) students I met while working on this book, using media connections and friendships I made with high school principals and various brains-behind-the-brawn secretaries, I was able to start an exchange program. As a result some fifty students got to know each other as people, not as rich kid-poor kid stereotypes.

I continued to learn about my false assumptions. One night I stayed up late talking with a girl, the president of her inner-city high school's National Honor Society, with whom I'd become good friends. "Where are you going to college next year?" I asked. "I'm not," she said. In disbelief I asked why not. "Because I want to become a cosmetologist," she said.

Or there was the night I asked the family I was staying with during the exchange, "How do you feel about me, that by a stroke of luck whatever work I do will go toward my being successful and prospering and whatever work you do is just for surviving?"

Afterword

"We accept that fact. We're proud of you. We don't feel sorry for ourselves," they said. "We have our life to live." They were so proud and had so much dignity, I was ashamed to have asked the question.

Still, those of us who worked on this book can't shake our sense of responsibility for the kids who shared their lives with us. We want to tell and retell their stories. "I sometimes feel that if anyone experienced what I did they couldn't help but feel responsible," says fellow editor Julie Horowitz. Tanya Pearlman says she's not sure how the experience has changed her, but that it was important to her to discover that there really is "a cord of humanity that can tie people together."

As for me, I now see myself as part of a great and diverse world which I have the responsibility and potential to change. The CHILDREN'S EXPRESS experience of communicating firsthand with people of divergent backgrounds has given me a new perspective.

Working on this book has made me realize that there are kids who have to resist incredible outside pressures just to remain in school. Also, there are kids who are not in school who have to forego a time of learning essential for their survival in later life because they have "more important" things to do. I now understand that potential dropouts and actual dropouts are not merely statistics; they are real people with fears, desires and dreams. They are real people who often have a lot to say—if only we would listen.

Teen Editor: Rachel Burg

Appendix

We would like to thank the following individuals and schools for participating in this project:

KANSAS CITY, MO.
Brian Ashely, 18
Delores Bass, 17
Alice Brown, 17
Christy Burnworth, 11
Ulisses Caraballo, 12
Lori Casper, 16
Joe Cowham, 17
Maureen Dreiling, 17
Candice Fisher, 14
Rick Gary, 18
Mathew Gillespie, 10
Mike Hansuld, 13
Monica Hansuld, 13
Monica Harris, 14
Treneice Horton, 13
David Isaiah, 14
Lanese Jackson, 19
Brandon John, 13
Marcus Jones, 11
Jason Kearney, 16
Ramadae Khalifah, 11
Deborah King, 14
Shelly Kinzle, 16
Marla Kirk, 12
Patricia Kumpt, 16
Richard Lewis, 11
Tillman McClunie II, 13
Dwayne McDaniel, 10
Bryan McGraw, 10
Tina Miller, 10
Mai Nguyen, 11
Desmond Northcutt, 13
Mana Palmobia, 15
Debbie Pickens, 17
Michael Pledge, 14
Ray Roseberry, 16
Natasha Stephen, 12
Jerry Titrus, 17
Brent Wade, 18
Ryan Wright, 11

EDUCATORS

University of Kansas (Lawrence, KS):
John Wright, *Professor*
Shawnee Missions Alternative Education Program:
Charles Jackard, *Principal*

Kansas City School District:
Steven Herst, *Director of Public Information*
Eugene Wolkey, *Associate Superintendent of Elementary Education*

Lincoln Academy:
Joan Caulfield, *Principal*

Central Senior High School:
Melvin Franklin, *Principal*

Woodland Elementary:
Nathan Crookshank, *Principal*

Border Star Elementary:
Jesse Kirksey, *Principal*

De La Salle Education Center:
Jim Dougherty, *Executive Director*
Clark Powell, *Principal*

DALLAS

Kim Austen, 13
Wade Bass, 13
Sam Bou, 11
Ada Chapa, 16
David Chien, 15
Leticia Cortes, 16
Shawn Cox, 15
John Flores, 15
Terri Harris, 15
Maurice Hill, 14
Chris Hobbs, 17
Patricia Hutcherson, 18
Rachene Jackson, 15
Aaron Kaka, 13
Rom Kan, 12
Kirvy Leador, 17
Elise Lewis, 16
Dominga Lira, 13
Michael Marino, 11
Melissa Matta, 19
Ernest Mendosa, Jr., 13
Jose Regalado, 11
Chris Rodriquez, 14
Israel Rodriquez, 15
Joel Salinas, 17

Appendix

Debra Taylor, 17
Johnny Trevino, 19
Nicole Warner, 13
Gordon Williams, 14
Teresa Woodard, 11

SCHOOOLS AND EDUCATORS

Sunset High School:
Richard Marquis, *Principal*
Ed Nozano, *Teacher*
Loritha Ogburn, *Teacher*,
Laura Watson, *Teacher*

J.L. Long Jr. High School:
Jose Cardenas, *Teacher*
Linda Granger, *Teacher*
Anita Johnson, *Teacher*
Ameilia King, *Teacher*
Sharon Morgan, *Teacher*
Jolanda Rodriques, *Teacher*

J.L. Long Middle School:
Janet Skinner, *Principal*

Hexter Elementary School:
Martha Lochner, *Principal*

Bryan Adaams High School:
Joel Pittman, *Prinicpal*

Alternative Career Center:
Robert Parrish, *Principal*
Don Whitehall

Dallas Independent School District School:
Dean Angel, *Communications*

OAKLAND

Mario Bermadez, 11
James Big Bear, 14
Art Boissiere, 15
Tyrone Bryant, 16
Natasha Campbell, 13
Suzette Chisolm, 16
Debbie Choy, 14
Ronico Colar, 16
Kalynn Colston, 11
Lisa Cotton, 15
Jada Dalbert, 11
Eric Dorris, 14
Ersie Everette, 18
Doyaughn Frierson, 16

Yang Kim, 14
Peter Kokot, 14
Bonnie Lee, 17
Ruby Lee, 16
Emery Lowe, 16
Heather McCardell, 15
Jonathon McDowell, 11
Michelle McDonald, 16
Sonjit Moore, 15
Lawrence Ruffin, 15
Daymon Simmons, 11
Glenn Stafford, 14
Ralph Westfield, 14
Katina Williams, 10

SCHOOLS AND EDUCATORS

Dewey High School:
Bob Goddard, *Teacher*
Richard Van Epps, *Teacher*
Bill Weed, *Teacher*

Longfellow Elementary School:
Don Thomas, *Principal*

Continuation Opportunities in Alternative Schools
Oakland Board of Education:
Fred Turner, *Program Manager*

Oakland High School:
Clifford O'Casey, *Principal*

McChessney Jr. High School:
David Swanson, *Principal*

Longfellow Elementary School:
Don Thomas, *Principal*

Castlemont High School:
Lee Nell Jennings, *Principal*

Dag Hammersjold Opportunity School:
Richard Griffin, *Principal*

Oakland Public Education Network:
Lou Ann Aaberg
Ann Katz
Loretta Straharsky

NEWARK

Jamell Austin, 15
Lakeenya Bennett, 13
Rosa Blez, 14
Ann Bowser, 17

Appendix

Mark Crockett, 17
Granger Darden, 15
Craig Dixon, 16
Sabrina Edwards, 17
Yolanda Ellison, 16
Amanda Fluellen, 18
Alphonso Gaillard, 17
Evelyn Gomez, 13
Katina Howard, 14
Margarita Irizarry, 13
Troy Johnson, 15
Mario Jones, 13
Nicole Jones, 16
Tanya Lawson, 17
Nicole Mintz, 17
Malinda Mottenon, 17
Anna Navarro, 16
Rosa Perez, 13
Wychie Reynolds, 13
Coleman Robinson, 15
Shakir Sharrieff, 19
Tyiesha Smalls, 18
Vernon Smallwood, 15
Raymond Stover, 17
Damaris Valentin, 13
Stacey Walker, 13
Donna Williams, 16
Robert Williams, 18
Tawanna Williams, 14
Rachel Winn, 16
Mark Winston, 16

SCHOOLS AND EDUCATORS

Newark Board of Education:
Bessie Morize, *Head of Secondary Guidance Education*

Avon Avenue School:
Lillian Gibson, *Principal*

McKinley School:
Louis Jorano, *Principal*
Susan Alvarez, *Guidance Counselor*

West Side High School:
Nathaniel Potts, *Principal*

Weequahic High School:
Lawrence Major, *Principal*

West Kinney Alternative School:
James Barrett, *Principal*
Helen Means, *Head Guidance Counselor*

BOSTON

Butch Bilodeau, 18
Lisa Bilodeau, 10
Angela Burke-Morton, 10
Shelby Bowling, 17
Shandolyn Cason, 17
Leticia Cruz, 8
Michael Dockery, 18
Carol Dunn, 14
Monnette Fung, 10
Dawn Gates, 14
Kelly E. Grimes, 10
Isaac Hampton, 10
Eric Harris, 10
Kirk Jiles, 19
Robert Jones, 17
Shawn Landry, 17
Hue Hoa Ly, 12
Marcie Mercure, 10
Delin Santo, 19
Michael Schnidler, 13
Lakeesha Stillwell, 10
Nahir Torres, 10
Paul Tu, 20
Terrence Tulloch, 17

SCHOOLS AND EDUCATORS

William Monroe Trotter School
Phyllis Wheatley Middle School
Boston Technical High School

Volunteers for Boston's Schools:
Betsy Nelson

Access Program:
Mario Pena

Josephine Chandler, *School Nurse*
Lynda Gordon, *Assistant Principal*
Dorothy Hasberry, *Substitute Teacher*
Mary Kennedy, *Speech Therapist*